Test Pattern

PLATE 1

Test Pattern

PLATE 2

Test Pattern

Test Pattern

PLATE 3

PLATE 3

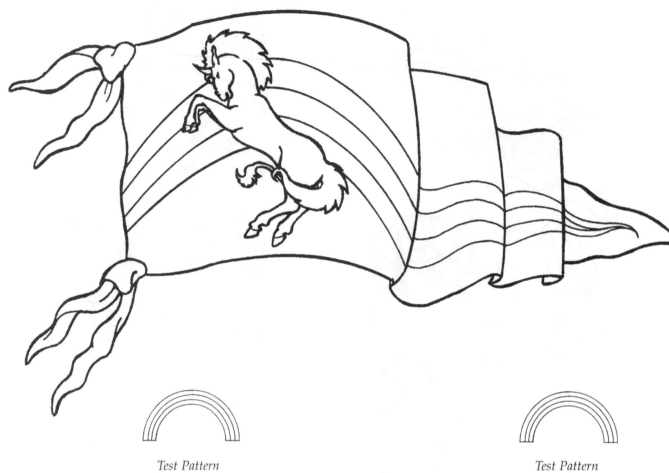

Test Pattern   *Test Pattern*

PLATE 4

PLATE 5

PLATE 5

Test Pattern

PLATE 6

Test Pattern

Test Pattern

PLATE 7

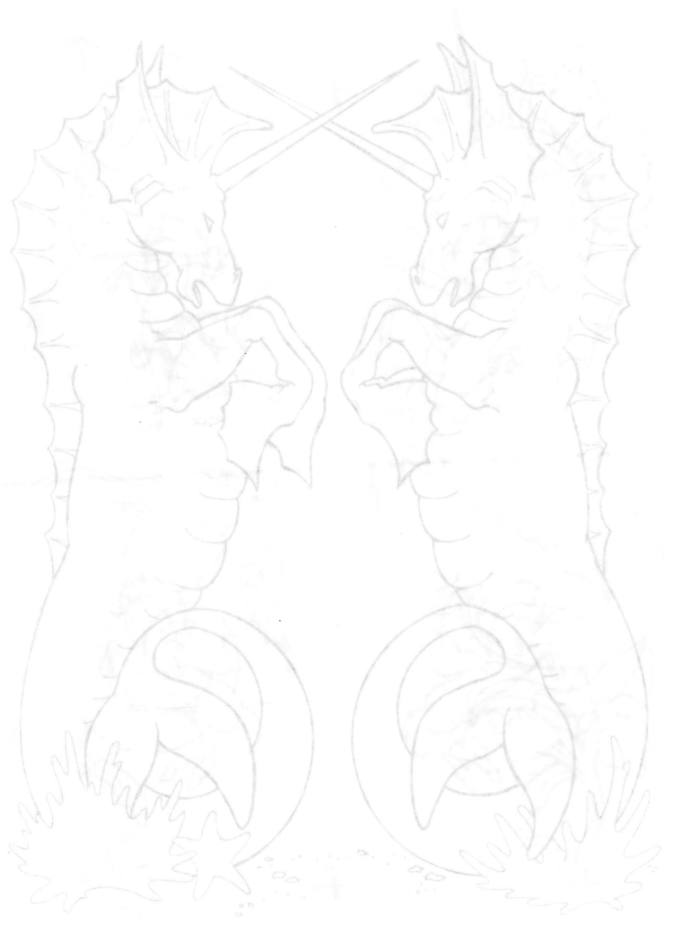

PLATE 8

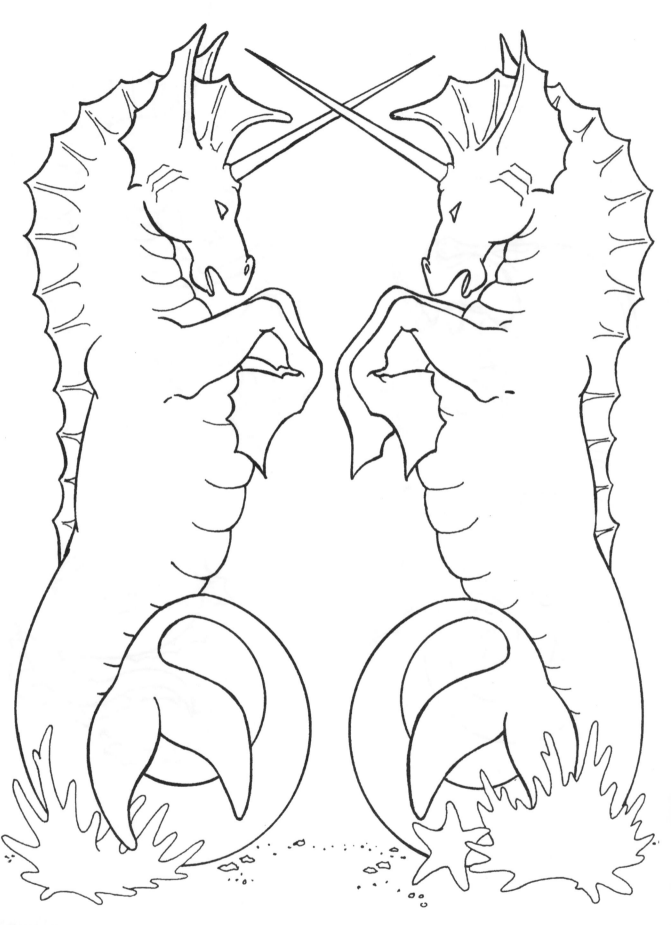

PLATE 8

Test Pattern

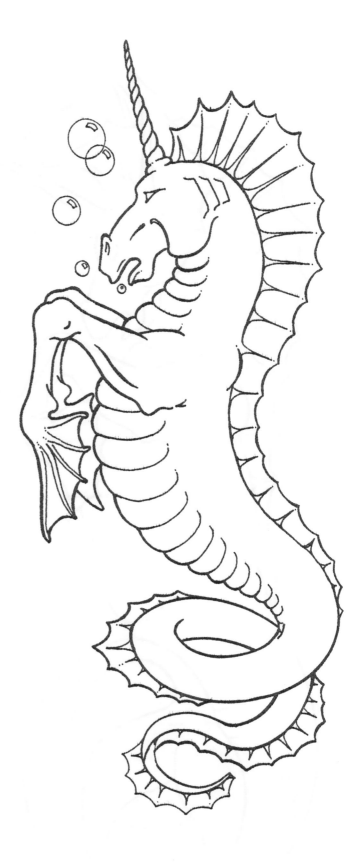

Test Pattern

PLATE 9

Test Pattern

PLATE 10

PLATE 11

Test Pattern

PLATE 12

PLATE 13

Test Pattern

PLATE 14

PLATE 15

PLATE 13

PLATE 16

Test Pattern

PLATE 17

PLATE 19

Test Pattern

PLATE 18

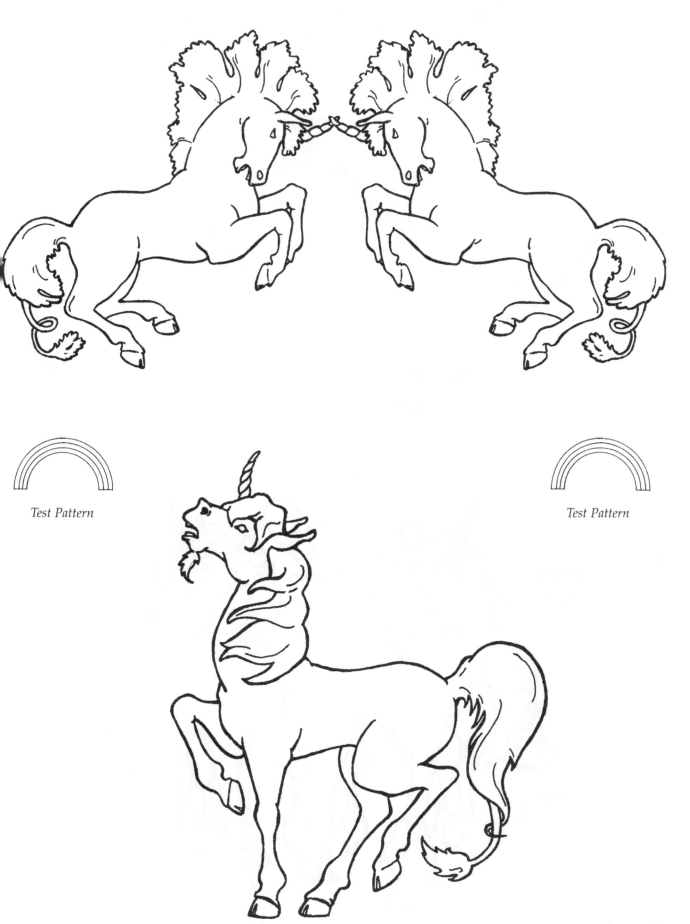

Test Pattern

Test Pattern

PLATE 19

PLATE 20

PLATE 20

PLATE 21

[PLATE 2]

PLATE 22

PLATE 22

Test Pattern

Test Pattern

Test Pattern

PLATE 23

PLATE 24

PLATE 24

B®ANDLife

Cafés & Coffeehouses

Integrated brand systems in graphics and space

"While branding may be just one component of a café's story, it's an important one. One that sets the tone of what you can expect when you step inside for that first cup of the day."

Post Projects

Alex Nelson, Partner & Creative Director

Cafés are – and have been for many years – a central hub of social life. More than just a place to re-caffeinate, they're a place to meet friends, review paperwork with a client, or complete that essay you've been putting off for too long. We go to cafés in part because we want to leave our houses but still feel like we're at home. They're a comforting routine. More intimate than a typical retail environment, they're smaller spaces with familiar faces and welcome predictable outcomes that connect a neighbourhood and local community.

Visiting a café is an experience that engages all the senses. In Vancouver BC, where our offices are based, new cafés are opening constantly. Sights, smells and tastes have to be carefully considered in order to stand out in such a competitive landscape. A well-thought-out visual identity and approach to branding is an important way to create some distinction – but not too well-thought-out. Fussy branding can feel uncomfortable and a café should be anything but.

Cafés tend to be highly personal expressions of their founders. They are more often than not small businesses with no more than a handful of locations and limited resources at their disposal. Creating an appropriate visual identity is therefore a sensitive and challenging task. Designers have to find creative ways to express a brand in atmosphere that has strong opinions and tight budgets in order to benefit both the owners and the public.

With these constraints in mind, a café identity has to account for exterior and interior signage, printed materials like packaging and menus, as well as digital deliverables in the form of a website and social media. All of these branded expressions have to then mesh well with the interior design of the space, which is often being done by another individual or agency.

Our job as designers is to assist in articulating that vision. In our experience at Post Projects, less tends to be more when it comes to branding cafés. Excessive branding can leave a space feeling impersonal or overly corporate. A visual identity is only one aspect of the whole experience. The interior design, the service and quality of the food and drinks, the location, the crowd, even the music, all come together alongside the branding to fully represent the vision the founders had in mind when they set out to open a café. A successful project will involve close dialogue between client, interior designer and branding agency. Sharing thoughts and ideas early in the process is helpful to ensure all parties are on the same page and working toward a cohesive idea.

BRANDLife: Cafés & Coffeehouses brings together a collection of world-class studios and their work for these spaces that are a home away from home for many of us. While branding may be just one component of a café's story, it's an important one. One that sets the tone of what you can expect when you step inside for that first cup of the day.

The Coffeevine

Alex Kitain, Founder

'Let's go get coffee, shall we?' —who hasn't used this phrase before? Well, unless you're a staunch tea drinker, maybe; but the truth is, even in countries where coffee is less common, the idea of getting together with friends, family or colleagues is still often associated with coffee.

From Mexico City to Tehran and from Amsterdam to Sydney, coffee is omnipresent. But these days, coffee is no longer just coffee. Over the past two decades, coffee has undergone an astonishing transformation from commodity to specialty, shining a completely new light on a product we all thought we knew.

Driven by a fast-growing community of producers, roasters, baristas and coffee consumers, specialty coffee is quickly becoming the norm across the world and frequently referred to as 'third wave'. This term refers to the current state of specialty coffee and its reincarnation as a carefully crafted product that has little in common with the coffee our parents grew up with.

We now have more access to sustainably sourced, beautifully roasted and expertly prepared specialty coffee than ever before. From inner city coffee roasters to spectacular coffee bars and from exciting coffee subscription services to ready-made coffee drinks, the world is rediscovering coffee on a whole new level and in a myriad of different ways. And more and more people are discovering that coffee can be a great ingredient in other products such as chocolate, beer or even in haute cuisine.

What is particularly striking is that even countries like Italy where espresso is king are gradually starting to discover lighter roasts, single origins and filter coffees. No one is safe from this delicious third wave of great coffee that is washing up on shores across the world.

In this book, we will explore some of the world's most spectacular coffee bars, roasteries, mixed retail spaces and coffee concepts that highlight the craftsmanship involved in serving that perfect cup of coffee.

About the author

Alex Kitain came into specialty coffee more by accident than by following ambition. After launching The Coffeevine as his personal guide to the best coffee bars in Amsterdam and beyond, he and his business partner Erica Armistead launched their critically acclaimed coffee subscription in 2014 with the aim to help more people discover and share truly great coffee. Kitain regularly contributes to leading coffee publications like Standart, Caffeine and Drift and makes sure that whenever he visits a new city, he makes a great coffee bar his first point of call. Now The Coffeevine is widely regarded as the most exciting and well-curated coffee box in Europe, enjoyed by coffee lovers the whole world over and deemed as the gold standard by many coffee roasters.

For more information visit www.thecoffeevine.com

"From exciting coffee subscription services to ready-made coffee drinks, the world is rediscovering coffee on a whole new level and in a myriad of different ways."

Contents

Over the years, coffee culture has come to establish itself as a bare necessity within our societal complex. This highly addictive cultural plague cultivates itself in the shape of cafés and coffeehouses all over the world, yet somehow retains the facade of a temple to many. Nevertheless, café culture today is no longer merely about the making of a well-brewed mug of coffee or a fulfilling slice of cake. We depend on these delectable temples to nourish our thirst for new and inspiring ways to experience casual dining. In two sections with focuses on brand applications and interior design, BRANDLife seeks to shed light on these identities which make up the crux of today's third wave coffee experiences.

Index of initials

Foreword

Cover story

Colby Barr, Verve Coffee Roasters
Eileen Hassi Rinaldi, Ritual Coffee Roasters

Showcase

Graphic Identities

Interiors & Architecture

Expert Talk

Visual Identity

Sabine Kernbichler & Nicole Lugitsch—moodley brand identity
Antti Hinkula—Kokoro & Moi

Interior Branding

Kylie Dorotic—We Are Huntly
Yova Yager—Kleyvdesign

Biography

VERVE

COFFEE ROASTERS

Dialogue with Co-founder
Colby Barr

Made in Santa Cruz, brick-and-mortar Verve Coffee Roasters has made a lasting impression upon the area's coffee shop scene. While Verve remains true to the Californian spirit, it also dedicates itself to the craft of coffee from "Farmlevel" all the way to "Streetlevel", effectively bridging the gap between seed and cup. This initiative is embedded within Verve's entire ethos but more importantly, it makes customers mindful about the impact they are making upon coffee culture when they visit. Currently with several shops around California and Tokyo, Verve is ardently striving to curate more tasteful and authentic coffee experiences around the world. Committed to both ethics and excellence, this unique specialty coffee shop is redefining standards within the arena of specialty coffee, a hallmark for the future of third-wave coffee culture.

Colby Barr & Ryan O'Donovan

Verve Coffee was co-founded by Colby Barr and Ryan O'Donovan, old college friends who share an undying passion for the art of coffee-making. While both contribute to the retail experience and overall brand direction for Verve, Barr acts as the green-coffee buyer and farmer liaison, whereas O'Donovan oversees roasting and product development. Not unlike many today, the two founders had fallen deeply in love with the practice and sought to channel these appetites into a coffee-roasting company now adored by many.

01

02

01-04_ Verve on West Third Street, Los Angeles.
Interior design by COMMUNE. Identity and
mural design by Colony.

How would you define today's new way of tasting and experiencing coffee? Why do you think this is so crucial to coffee culture?

On a professional level, the new way of tasting and evaluating coffee is to look for the attributes as opposed to the defects. This is emphasised in the niche end of coffee that we operate in where we are looking for the absolute best coffees in the world — coffees that are often unique and limited and have to truly be discovered.

I believe this is crucial to coffee culture because it puts an emphasis on quality. This focus on quality is really the only way that we can create an impact on producers. We can pay producers more if we charge more for their coffee, which we will only do if the coffee is exceptional. It's full circle. Welcome to Verve.

What was your initial vision when opening Verve?

When my business partner, Ryan O'Donovan and I opened Verve, we wanted to be the best coffee company in the world. We never thought anyone would really care or notice but we gave it everything we had since day one and have always strived to be the best. Fortunately enough people did care. Never underestimate your clientele.

What are your thoughts on LA's coffee shop scene? How did you hope Verve would stand out within or reinvent it?

LA is an amazing city. They say it is really a collection of villages and I get that. It is very neighbourhood-driven and has an eclectic population of people that are largely driven by aspiration. This dreamy, quality-of-life population has a great appetite for design, fashion, and food — including coffee.

The scene in Los Angeles is in its early stages. There are amazing places to get coffee and people are doing really interesting things, but in such a large place there is always room for more. Our goal was to enter a market with like-minded people and just do what we do best. Our focus on quality coffee, food, design and service is what we have led the way with and what has been making us successful. We really care.

What was the main idea behind opening a collaborative store with Juice Served Here in LA?

Our first LA store was indeed a collaboration with Juice Served Here. I actually met Alex Matthews, their CEO and co-founder when I first started looking at spaces before either of us had a lease, and before they technically existed. We really saw eye-to-eye on so many things business and personal, and when we shared the behind the scenes of our brands we knew we had to work together. There was just such synergy aesthetically and ethos-wise. The concept of coffee and juice in LA was also something we both believed in and that we wanted to showcase in a lifestyle-driven space.

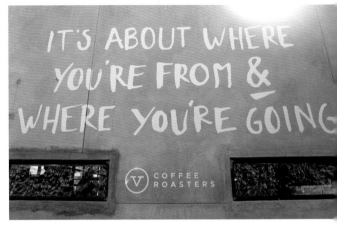

04

How has each of your individual backgrounds in the coffee industry fueled and informed the concept for Verve?

Ryan and I both love coffee. That's how this all began. Ryan has been a working coffee guy since he was 17 and often roasts coffee at home on his porch. He was my first "coffee geek" friend. He brought a real passion for the craft of the barista and the roaster to the game. Still does.

My background was a little different in that I grew up farming pears and wine grapes in Northern California so I took to green coffee buying. I have travelled around four months every year since we opened, establishing our relationships at origin.

Ryan and I share a passion for all things retail, design, marketing, and culture building, and contribute equally towards that. Our brand and our people are everything.

How do you communicate your 'Farmlevel meets Streetlevel' work ethic within the coffee shop? To what extent do you think graphic and interior branding helps reinforce this message?

"From Farmlevel to Streetlevel" is a message we are always pushing. A lot of it is subtle in how we name coffees after their farmers, segregate the branding of blends and single-origin coffees, and reinforce our staff in the education department. They are always learning about new coffees so they are a great resource to our customers.

Visual and interior branding are really important and are something we are expanding on as we grow. We were always gun-shy about communicating "Coffee geek talk" to people. We never wanted to come off as pretentious or accidentally turn people off with too much information. Now I think people are ready for more and we are looking for ways to offer them that access. We did just publish our first Farmlevel Digest (vol. 1: Honduras) which features our Direct Trade project in Honduras. It was shot on film by Ryan and I and is the first of a series, available for purchase online and in our stores. People are digging them.

In what ways does the atmosphere of Verve Coffee Roasters reflect the Californian character?

Our approach to retail design is pretty light and airy, yet warm and inviting. We love natural light and natural materials. We have more of a residential approach to our buildout than a commercial one. We want it to feel like an amazing kitchen rather than an industrial food service place. We want it to be aspirational yet relatable. A lot of our residential influences come from California designers including Charles and Ray Eames, Mickey Muennig and Commune Design. Commune was behind the design of two of our LA locations, on Third Street and Melrose Avenue.

What makes your tools and methods of roasting coffee different to other artisanal coffee shops?

We kind of have a yin-and-yang approach to our coffee roasting in that we are heavy with technology and the hand. All of our coffees are roasted by hand without automation on vintage German roasters, and each coffee is roasted using its own uniquely developed roast profile. Every coffee is tasted and scored every day, without knowing which coffee is which. This is called "blind" tasting.

That said, we use computers to track the temperature curves of every single batch we roast and log it to a unique roast ID. Each coffee is also measured by a laser colour analyser to ensure consistency.

We can look back at these quantifiable measurements and link them to our qualitative ones to better understand what is happening and to make sure our coffees are consistent.

With the development of new technologies and increased accessibility, many are now able to make great-tasting coffee at home. What then would you say makes Verve Coffee essential to the experience of coffee-lovers?

What makes Verve Coffee essential is that by buying our coffees you are not only guaranteed to be drinking the best coffees on Earth but are also doing good by supporting higher premiums paid to those producers for their exceptional work. It's the driving force of our Farmlevel Initiative: Ethics & Excellence.

You have recently opened a shop in Shinjuku, Japan. Why Japan? What do you think is the core difference between coffee culture in Japan and in California?

Japan was something that we have always dreamed of at Verve. There is a cosmic connection between California and Japan. They are very inspired by the California lifestyle and it informs a lot of their fashion and design. It's actually very cool. In fact they may do California better than we do!

We were very fortunate to be approached for our location in Shinjuku. It is an incredible neighbourhood and is in a bit of transition. It kind of reminds me of downtown LA in that way. It is very busy, vibrant and endlessly interesting.

The coffee scene in Japan is very established. It is a big part of their culture and they are so detailed and precise in their approach to it. I feel that this niche end of coffee that Verve exists in is very young but growing fast. If I was looking for a core difference between Japan and California it is that most of the shops there are very, very small and owner-operated on the daily.

What are your goals and hopes for the future? With Verve's expansion, has it been difficult to ensure you consistently produce authentic and fair-trade specialty coffee?

Our dreams for the future are strangely enough the same as they were when we opened; to create the best coffee experience we possibly can for our customers, our staff, and our producers. By staying focused on quality, growth simply allows us to share our experience with more people in this coffee chain. It's win-win for everybody — from Farmlevel to Streetlevel.

05-06_Verve's work ethic is subtly reinforced in its coffee packaging. Identity designed by Colony.
07-08_Verve on Melrose Avenue, Los Angeles. Interior design by COMMUNE.

07

08

"By staying focused on quality, growth simply allows us to share our experience with more people in this coffee chain. It's win-win for everybody — from Farmlevel to Streetlevel."

12

09, 12_Verve's Pacific Avenue store in Santa Cruz. Interior design by fuse architects Inc.
10_Cold brewed coffee on nitro-tap at Verve's Melrose Avenue store
11_Verve merchandise at its Downtown Los Angeles store

RITUAL
COFFEE

Dialogue with Owner & Founder
Eileen Hassi Rinaldi

Over a decade ago, Ritual Coffee Roasters opened their flagship shop in the Bay Area, a time when specialty coffee had not yet gained much traction. Today, Ritual has expanded to five different locations and made a significant impression upon San Francisco's coffee scene. Emphasising the importance of coffee consciousness is a central value to Ritual's identity. Through honest practice of sourcing, roasting and brewing, their dedication to spreading awareness about artisanal coffee is scrupulous. Ritual has also consistently adapted and progressed with the culture of the times, recently developing a new brand. Their original militant-looking red logo accurately represented their aggressive entry into the coffee scene in 2005, when it was crucial to make a bold statement. However today, with a developed loyalty within their customer base and an already changed state of coffee culture, their new identity requires a friendlier and more trusting appearance, manifested in the fresh and organic gold and white palette.

Eileen Hassi Rinaldi

Eileen Hassi fell in love with the coffee business during her first job as a manager at a coffeehouse. Interacting with people every day, making coffee for customers and managing staff were just a few things that attracted her to the industry. When she met David Schomer, CEO of Espresso Vivace, he served her a cup of coffee that essentially changed her life. This moment of revelation provoked her to learn more about the art of specialty coffee, preparing her for the success that is Ritual Coffee Roasters.

"Having fun and taking the coffee seriously continue to be a part of the culture, but now I know that creating a great work environment is critical to being sustainable in the long run."

How would you define the new way of tasting and experiencing coffee today? Why do you think this is so crucial to coffee culture?

Coffee is simply better now than it was 15 years ago. It's better at all the levels: green coffee, roasting, preparation. The quality of green coffee is better — it's packaged better, gets here faster, and is less likely to be compromised during transport. At the preparation level, there has been a stronger focus on proper extraction, using more sophisticated tools and equipment, and acquiring a better understanding of the chemistry of coffee. All of these lead to more transparency in roast. We can roast lighter now that the coffee is better. This has completely changed the customer experience — people can now taste the difference between mediocre and outstanding coffee. It's something people can get excited about. I know for everyone who works at Ritual, there was a day when a really good cup of coffee changed their life. That happens for our customers too!

What was your initial vision when opening Ritual in San Francisco?

I wanted to give the people of San Francisco the coffee they deserved. In 2004, the only style of coffee in the Bay Area was super dark roasted and there was no transparency about where it was from. On the contrary, people paid attention to where their meat came from and who grew their vegetables. People cared about heirloom varieties of fruits and vegetables. Coffee simply wasn't on the same level. I wanted to create a café that provides delicious coffee in a comfortable environment with fun baristas. I wanted to create a community. I wanted to raise the bar for coffee. I'm excited because we did it, and we will keep doing it!

How have your goals changed from the initial stages of Ritual Coffee and in what ways has it stayed the same?

From the very early stages, if we were having a hard time making a decision, we would ask ourselves whether that would make the coffee taste better. If the answer is yes, we would do it. That hasn't changed. We still ask ourselves what we can do to improve our coffee's taste *all* the time.

What has changed is that I'm more focused on making Ritual an outstanding place to work. When we were new, everything was exciting because we were pioneers. Having fun and taking the coffee seriously continue to be a part of the culture, but now I know that creating a great work environment is critical to being sustainable in the long run.

What changes have you witnessed within San Francisco's coffee culture since 2005?

It was unrecognisable. Back then we were the only game in town. We got to shock people every day with how good the coffee could be. Now San Francisco is known worldwide as a great coffee destination where people expect to find the best coffee. There are four or five places to get amazing coffee just on Valencia Street alone. New roasters pop up all the time.

What inspired the coffee shop's name 'Ritual'?

I drink coffee every day. Drinking my first coffee is the only thing I do every day that feels... sacred. It is a special moment when you put the warm cup to your lips. Every day is full of opportunity, and having coffee will just make it better. It feels like a ritual to me. So when I was picking a name, I kept coming back to the word "ritual". To me, it conveys that coffee is something special and sacred. Not just a habit or a necessity.

Ritual opened more than a decade ago when specialty coffee was not yet widely recognised. In those initial stages, how were you able to convey your values to customers most convincingly?

The first thing we do was to get them to drink the coffee. We had to gain people's trust, which we did by giving them something delicious, that they'd never had before. Once they tasted it and wanted to talk about how they found it different, we were excited to have those conversations. We were enthusiastic, we were earnest, and above all, we were passionate about it. That resonated with people, apparently.

01

02

03

04, 08-09_ Ritual's new identity aims to make
the brand more approachable.
05_ New packaging adds belly band, detailing the
bean's origin, harvest date and roast date.
06_ Ritual's original café and flagship on Valencia
Street, San Francisco

04

06

05

08

09

What role do you think Ritual played in the growth of today's new brand of coffee culture?

We brought it to San Francisco and Napa. I believe that it has spread from both places because these places are constantly looking to us for ideas and inspiration. Plus, a ridiculous number of influential people in the coffee world has cut their teeth at Ritual. I'm proud of that!

What are some key components that have changed as a result of Ritual's rebranding?

The rebranding is mostly a response to the changes in coffee culture. When we first opened, we were doing something that was completely unfamiliar to people. We had to get people's attention and let them realise what we did was different. Eleven years in, people know what we're about and they trust us. We can stop yelling so much.

Has remodeling the coffee shop served to refine Ritual's mission? How crucial do you think remodeling was to updating Ritual's identity?

The Valencia Street Ritual is our original café, and it's our flagship. We didn't expect a line out the door within a matter of days of opening. We could not have predicted the overwhelming success, the need for two espresso machines in one shop and so many baristas working.

In 2005, when we opened, there was nothing like Ritual in San Francisco. We were the only 1,800-square-foot café that served only coffee and pastries, not food. In 2013, we remodelled. This gave us a chance to fix all of those mistakes that we made from underestimating how much people appreciated our work. It also gave us a chance to make the café a reflection of the quality we aspired to have. We have some of the best coffee in the world, and our original cafés frankly did not reflect that. With the remodelling, our space communicates that we take the quality of the coffee seriously.

In the decade of Ritual's lifetime, are there any milestones or challenges faced that have greatly impacted your trajectory?

The single biggest thing that has impacted our trajectory is that incredible people have been drawn to Ritual — and that has been the biggest surprise. Before our first brick-and-mortar store opened, passionate baristas found us and said that they wanted to come work at Ritual, to be a part of what we were doing. That is still happening. And without these incredibly smart, dedicated and passionate people, Ritual would not be the company that it is today. I'm so grateful for all of the people whose fingerprints are all over Ritual.

Graphic Identities

Visualising brand in print

b & b
Belle Epoque
Cafe Decada
Cafe Diego
Cafe for the Good Day
Coffee & Co.
Coffee & Kitchen
Dollop Coffee & Tea
Fazer Café
Hotel Daniel Bakery
Keisari Bakery
Le Batinse
Le Marché Cafe
Leckerbaer
Lune Croissanterie
MAISON
Mangolds
Matamata
MiddleState Coffee
Monjo Coffee

NORTHSHORE
OFF-GRID CAFÉ Physical
OKTOKKI The Café
Operator 25 Café
Pablo & Rusty's Coffee Roasters
PANTONE CAFE
Paseo Colón
Revolver Coffee
Ritaru Coffee
Sorry Coffee Co.
Stone Way Café
The Flour Pot Bakery
The Gardens Table Organic Café
The Local Mbassy
The Tannery Café
Tostado Café Club
Vete-Katten
Voyageur du Temps
Yardstick Coffee

Identities are as inherent to individuals as they are to businesses. They embody more than just an outward impression; through identities, we come to realise an entity's story, vision and values. When a brand builds a successful graphic identity, it seeps into the veins of our consumer-based society and demands to be realised. Upon noticing a cafe's logo brandished on a paper cup, it is not only the attractive design or colour scheme that we recognise, but the principles and services that the brand stands for. It structurally unites a cafe's unique qualities with societal expectations, leaving behind visual memories that keep us coming back for more.

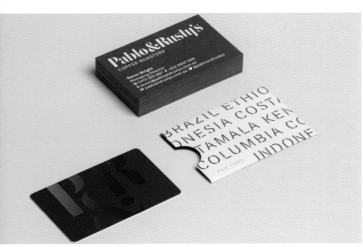

Pablo & Rusty's
Coffee Roasters

Sydney, Australia

ID Manual   **IN** Giant Design   **PH** Andrew Worssam   **CL** Pablo & Rusty's Coffee Roasters

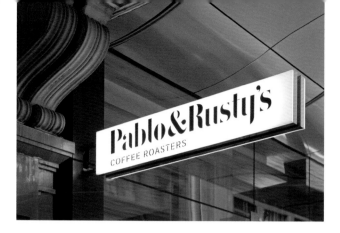

In seeking to better exemplify their values of sustainable practice and authenticity, Pablo and Rusty's decided to remodel their brand's identity with Manual. Knowing that the café is colloquially referred to as 'P&R', Manual adopted this already fashionable nickname and incorporated it into a new monogram, which works well as van livery and as corporate stamps on sugar packaging and staff uniform. Inspired by stencil letterings commonly found on coffee sacks and assuming an elegant white and blue palette, a refreshing visual identity is revealed which is aesthetically minimal yet of high quality and sophistication. Their monogram and logotype are scattered across the collateral, imbibing customers into the brand's sense of simplicity and utility, ultimately distinguishing itself from the visual vernacular found in many of today's coffee shops.

Mangolds

Graz, Austria

ID moodley brand identity   **CL** Mangolds

Being one of the first vegetarian restaurants in Graz, Austria, Mangolds promotes itself as a leading dining destination for fresh and healthy foods. After deciding to rebrand with Moodley, the restaurant's identity more effectually counters the stigma on vegetarian food that considers it boring or bland. The Mangolds logo uses a mix of bold typefaces, which revives the jovial atmosphere of the restaurant and the varied selection of foods they provide. This playing with colours, fonts and typefaces is also prominent in the restaurant's interior, where their sign boards, menus and merchandise all have similar flairs in design.

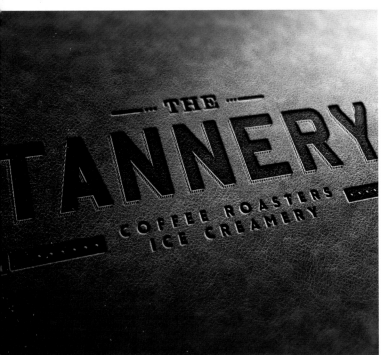

The Tannery Café

Auckland, New Zealand

ID 485 Design   **IN** Material Creative   **CL** Mt. Atkinson Coffee and Kohu Road Ice-cream

A collaboration between Mt. Atkinson Coffee and Kohu Road Ice-cream, The Tannery Café's brand identity acknowledges the goodness of combos and builds upon duality. Just as "good things come in pairs", like ice-cream and coffee, the brand campaign is based around matching pairs or expressions with their opposite meanings, which is manifested across their logo and poster art. The hand-painted signage at the storefront and leather cup coasters are attributed to the building's former tenant, one of the first leather tanneries in town. A wall separating the roasting room from the tasting area features diagonally laid wood panels mimicking mountain imagery, juxtaposed with loft-style windows inspired by Mt. Atkinson Coffee's logo and Kohu Road's factory.

NORTHSHORE

Osaka, Japan

ID ZEALPLUS   **IN** Kazuki Sumioka   **PH** Kazufumi Nakamura
SE (Metalwork) Yamazaki Rie, (Plants) Enoki Atsushi   **ST** Hitomi Nakamura   **CL** Hanafru

A transliteration of the Kitahama district of Osaka where this Hawaiian-themed café is located, the name 'NORTHSHORE' retains a familiarity for its local audience. Along with the wood-clad interior, neon signage and surfboard logo that are reminiscent of the laidback, carefree atmosphere of the Hawaiian coast, ZEALPLUS designs a restaurant that embraces both local and foreign tendencies. The use of raw, earthy elements and greenery in the identity and space design also help construct a brand that is organic and health-inspired.

COFFEE & ESPRESSO

NORTHSHORE BLEND / TODAYS COFFEE /
LATTE / CAPPUCCINO / AFFOGATO

FRUIT TEA

LEMON / APPLE / PINEAPPLE / LA FRANCE / GRAPE

RASPBERRY / FRAMBOISE

COLD PRESSED JUICE

KALE DIET / CIRCLE / REPAIR / RED BEATS

WHITENING / WARM UP / REFRESH / ENERGY

Fazer Café

Helsinki, Turku, Tampere & Vaasa, Finland

ID Kokoro & Moi   **IN** Koko3, Kokoro & Moi   **CL** Fazer

Established in 1891, Fazer Café is considered to be one of Helsinki's finest and most longstanding cafés. Kokoro Moi strove to encapsulate the strong and timeless essence of this local gem by striking a balance between sophistication and comfort. This balance is most candidly demonstrated by the contrasts within their blue, gold and yellow palette, which elegantly embraces the café's double-edged character. Drawing their forms from the classic 'Fazer' sign in Kluuvikatu Street, Fazer Grotesk and Fazer Chisel are two cornerstone typefaces used comprehensively to tie Fazer Café's new visual identity together. This rigid and authoritative font is utilised in everything from the logo, menu boards, packaging, to clothing, to wall decor.

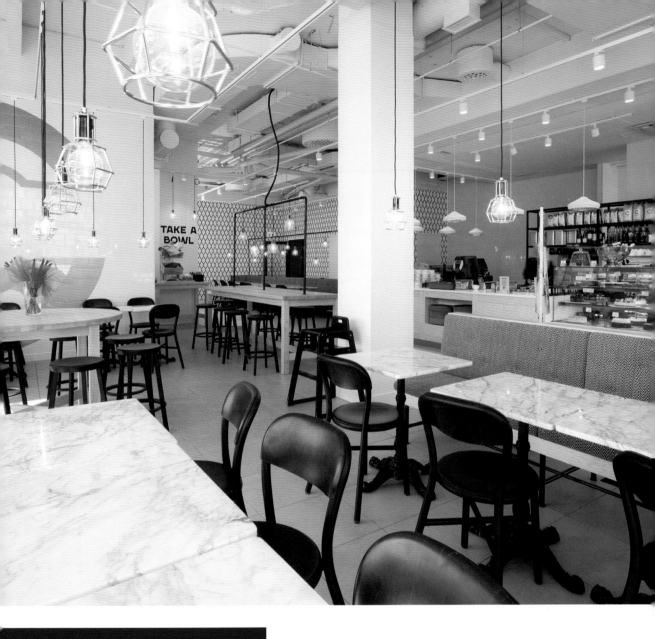

OVE AT
RST BITE.

Fazer

CAFÉ

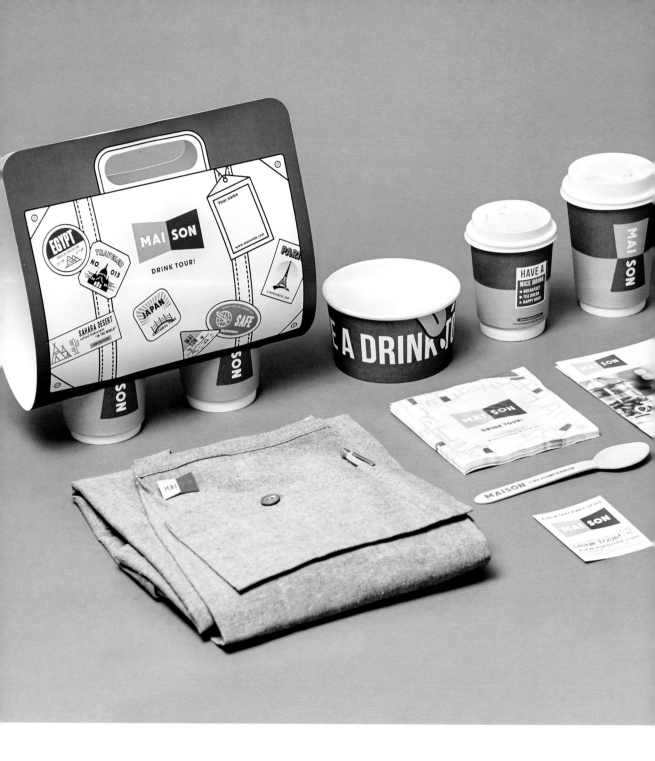

MAISON

Yuen Long, Hong Kong

ID Way of Difference Ltd.   **IN** Oft Interior   **PH** Tsz Chun Leóncio Lai / The Buffacow   **CL** MAISON HK

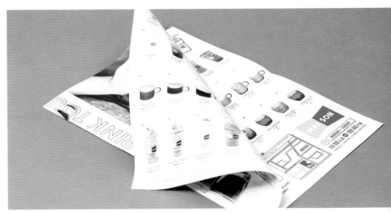

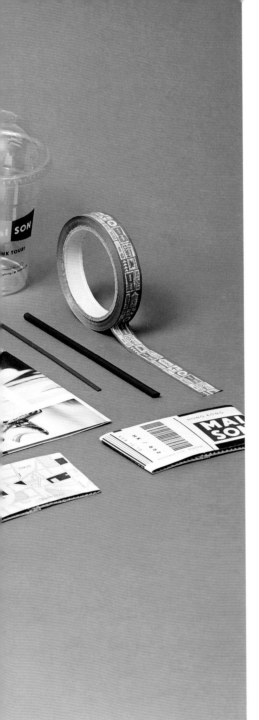

Fusing regional flavours into their floral tea recipes, MAISON hopes that its patrons can embark on a new journey with every sip of tea. An airport terminal theme, indicating the starting point of every adventure, is integral to the brand concept. From its take-away packaging designed to resemble security labels and a well-travelled suitcase, to the interior clad in country codes, coordinates, arrival signs and wayfinding signage, this idea runs seamlessly throughout the shop. On top of that, most drinks are named to impart the local tea-drinking habit of different locations, such as "Hong Kong 3:15". The trapezoids in MAISON's logo signify the wings of airplanes while a delightful palette adds an exuberant, youthful spirit to empower every tea experience.

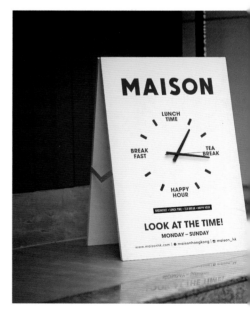

PANTONE CAFE

Larvotto, Monaco

ID Giraudi Group

PANTONE ECLAIR
13-0221
Pistachio Green

As catering group Giraudi's very first venture into the dining sector, PANTONE CAFE opened its first pop-up bistro in Monaco for two months in 2015. Playing on Pantone's theme, the café invited patrons to "taste the colour". From sandwiches and chocolate éclairs to water, every product sold at the café was colour-coded and labelled akin to Pantone's original colour identification system, enabling each colour to carry its own distinct personality. The café's setting and packaging designs were stripped down to a minimal and uniform format coherent to the brand's signature colour swatch design, overall creating a multisensory experience that combines the pleasures of sight with the pleasures of taste.

PANTONE
CAFE

PANTONE Soft Drinks

#PANTONECAFE

PANTONE C
18-1763
Red Grin

PANTONE ECLAIR
19-1625
Decadent Chocolate

PANTONE
15-1049

PANTONE
14-4810
Carlat Blue

PANTONE
VERSE™

Design * Michel Penneman
Architect * A2M
Think Tank *
Photo * Vendredi spri * Designerfarbur

PANTONE
U N I V E R S E
14-0756 TCX   Empire Yellow

PANTONE CAFE
18-1763
Red Grimaldi Forum

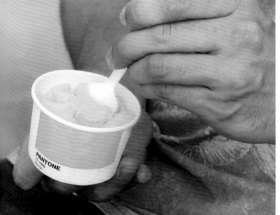

PANTONE
U N I V E R S
18-2133
Pink Flamb

Lune Croissanterie
Melbourne, Australia

ID A Friend of Mine   **IN** Studio Esteta   **PH** Tom Blachford   **SE** (Lighting) BREC   **CL** Lune Croissanterie

LUNE

Beginning as a tiny shop in Melbourne's suburb, Lune Croissanterie wanted a comprehensive revamp after outgrowing its previous branding and store. Local design studio A Friend of Mine was responsible for the brand's graphic update. Aligning with the bakery's name, the new logotype has kept the much loved rocket motif while adding a croissant twist and subtle glitter print to channel a playful spirit on the packaging. A hyperdrive pattern remarkably completes the lune-inspired galactic theme, bringing about the die cut ventilation slots on the takeaway boxes, the splayed LED lights inside the glass-walled working space and motion graphics on Lune's website. Part of the warehouse quality was retained to contrast the transparent shrine, where patrons can view the bakers' craft while they eat or wait for their pastries.

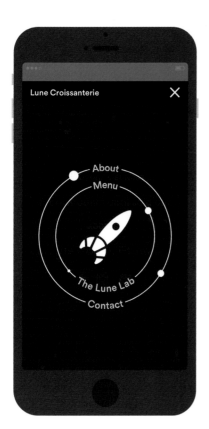

The Local Mbassy

Sydney, Australia

ID Korolos   **IN** (Design) Korolos, (Drafting) Yelena Smetannikov   **PH** Shayben Moussa
SE (Installation) David Haines @Lunatiques, (Mural) Sid Tapia   **CL** Marcus Gorge

From its 1920s music playlist to its made-to-measure furnishings, The Local Mbassy commends local hooligans and revolutionaries for moulding Australia's art and coffee culture. Boiler-room aesthetics flow through the café's space, juxtaposing exposed-pipe fittings with antiques, leather bike-pedal stools, and street art by local artist Sid Tapia to enrich the tone. Applied on a cardboard stock simply with black ink, rubber stamps and blind embossing, the logo of two profile silhouettes echoes the theme and gives off a retro touch. Wooden table tops, chairs and menu covers add warmth and round off the concept with refined craftsmanship.

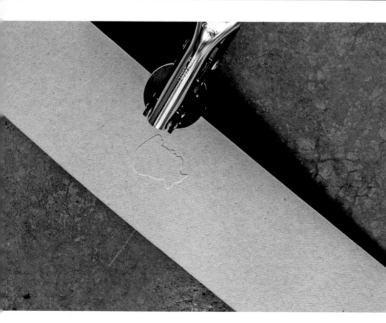

The Gardens Table
Organic Café

Sydney, Australia

ID Judit Besze   **CL** The Gardens Table Organic Café

The Garden Table offers organic, old-fashioned food in Sydney. Drawn to the heavenly setting of a "secret garden", graphic designer Judit Besze took exotic botanic patterns as core graphic elements and created a captivating world of passion flower tendrils, coffee beans and hummingbirds across the café's packaging and stationery. The fine and colourful illustrations were counterbalanced by plenty of white space to give each branded surface some room to breathe. Their brown paper bag, adorned by simple graphics and a three-lined logotype, keeps in line with The Garden Table's commitment to serving only clean and natural food.

Coffee Roasters

—

Coffee roasters are widely regarded as one of the most crucial elements of the coffee supply chain. Not just because this is where the finishing touches are applied to each bean, but also because many of them are deeply involved in the production of coffee at origin.

The idea that even a relatively small coffee roastery can have such a great impact on the quality of its product by developing close ties with farmers was pioneered by the likes of Stumptown and Counter Culture in the USA. Their thinking was simple but it changed the coffee industry.

By visiting their farmers every year, sharing knowledge and insights with them, reinvesting parts of their profit in communal and infrastructure projects, and most importantly, by paying a much higher amount for their coffees than was the norm, these roasters developed a standard that is today referred to as 'Direct Trade'.

As a result, over the years, many other roasters began to follow suit and those who have worked with the same farms for some years have been able to continuously improve the quality of their coffees.

Naturally, this has also paved the way for many highly respected green coffee traders who act on behalf of smaller roasters for whom direct trade is too costly.

Back in the day, coffee roasters used to be hidden away in industrial terrains, usually far outside of the city's bustling core; but these days you can find spectacular coffee roasteries in every hip neighbourhood. Indeed, some roasters have expanded their stores to include their own cafés, restaurants or bars, and have effectively taken their production work right to the customer.

Gone are the days when one could only buy coffee from local supermarkets and learn next to nothing about the product itself. Coffee roasters and coffee bars now regularly offer trainings and workshops, and their outlets act as a showroom where anyone can ask questions, learn about the product and discover that coffee is not just coffee.

Even huge multinational coffee chains like Starbucks have realised that they were missing out on a unique point of contact with consumers and have begun to open spectacular roasting and retail spaces like the Reserve Roastery in Seattle.

List of some inspiring coffee roasting spaces

Allpress, London | Blue Bottle, Tokyo | Four Barrel, San Francisco | Starbucks Reserve, Seattle
Stooker Roasting Co, Amsterdam | The Barn, Berlin | The Coffee Collective, Copenhagen
The Village Coffee & Music, Utrecht

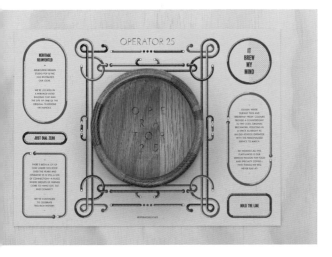

Operator 25 Café

Melbourne, Australia

ID Pop & Pac   **PH** Mark Lobo   **CL** Operator 25 Café

Operator 25 sits in a building previously home to Melbourne's first telephone exchange. Striving for a seamless marriage between contemporary design and digital heritage, Pop & Pac drew on the patterns and layouts of telephone switchboards to develop a new visual identity for the café. By cleverly associating streamlined cords and connection holes with Roy Lichtenstein's renowned Ben-Day dots, Operator 25 presents an aesthetic that alludes to the cadences of speech. The café's bold artwork, unique typefaces and witty messages combine to form a refreshing and lighthearted atmosphere that effectively translates antiquated forms of communication into catalysts for modern design.

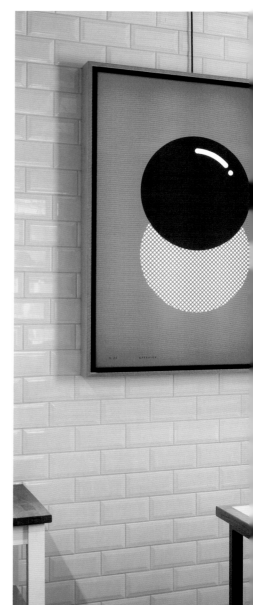

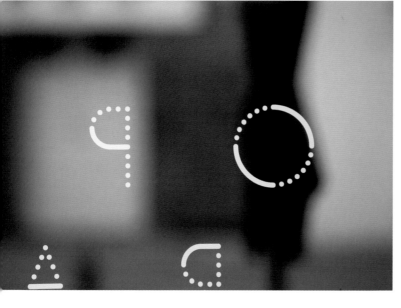

Le Marché Cafe

Miami, USA

ID Jiani Lu   **CL** Le Marché Cafe

Le Marché Cafe is a gourmet café inspired by traditional Parisian design. Featuring warm wooden flairs, impressive textures and rustic urban accents, the space's interior propagates a cosy and stylish setting. Jiani Lu sought to develop a brand identity, collateral design and menu board that evoke a feeling of warmth and happiness. This is reflected in a red-orange palette used in collaterals, which nicely contradicts the earthy, neutral tones of the interior. Lu produced three variations of the logo, which feature a typeface that strikes a balance between the aesthetics of vintage labels and modern sans serif fonts. She also customised the accent on the letter 'E' in the logo and 'M' in the monogram — a signature component that offers a delicate calligraphic touch to Le Marché Cafe's identity.

Paseo Colón

Lima, Peru

ID Infinito Consultores   **IN** Jorge Balerdi   **CL** Mambrino SAC

del **BOTICARIO**
✳ RECETA ✳ ✳ COMPLETA ✳

• MOJITO •
Ron blanco, zumo de limón, agua con gas y machacado
de hierba buena con azúcar.   S/. 16.=

• CHILCANO DE PISCO •
Pisco Queirolo, zumo de limón, ginger ale y gotas
de amargo de angostura.   S/. 14.=

• MARGARITA FICHA •
Tequila Cuervo 1800 Reposado, Comtreau y lime juice.   S/. 22.=

• CUBA LIBRE •
Ron Bacardí añejo, Coca Cola y zumo de limón.   S/. 15.=

• PISCO PUNCH •
de piña golden y zumo de limón.   S/. 15.=

hirly Cherries, granadina
con jugo de naranja,
y ginger ale.
S/. 10.=

PASEO COLON
CAFE

Paseo Colón sought to immerse its Latin-American essence into the sophistication of contemporary design. Infinito developed this remembrance for colonial heritage through the incorporation of old-style photography on menus, coasters and wall art, tinted with an invigorating turquoise blue to give it that vibrant modern flair, as well as to resonate with the psychedelic quality of Latin-American folk art. Of particular interest is the cafe's logo, where the contours of the typeface and use of gold colour beautifully resonate with the strain of simple and solid architectural constructions through Latin America's colonial period. Infinito achieves an identity for Paseo Colón that cohesively harmonises cultural heritage with modern aesthetics.

Le Batinse

Quebec CIty, Canada

ID Deux et Quatre   **IN** Perron Design   **CL** Le Batinse

Intrinsic to the undeniably unique atmosphere of Le Batinse is its fusing of old-school and modern-day trends. Inspired by retrospective design, Deux et Quatre elevates the comfortable, homemade attributes of 'grandma' cuisine and decor to a level which meets the aesthetic fashion of today. Through the use of vintage hyperrealistic floral illustrations and a delightfully utopian colour palette in the presentation of menus, stationery, furnishings and even food and drinks, this restaurant's branding identity effectually brings about an atmosphere that is warm and comfortable, yet vibrant and sublime. Le Batinse has become a sanctuary of style and comfort within the historic neighbourhood of Old Quebec.

Cafe for the Good Day

Minoh, Japan

ID 6B   **IN** Cafe for the Good Day, 6B   **PH** (Poster) Shohei Tanaka @Shohei Tanaka Photo Studio
CL Cafe for the Good Day   **CR** Hide Kosugi @VVVV

Cafe for The Good Day transmits touches of joy and bliss through the coffee cup, urging you to relish life's great pleasures within a romantic setting. Large cyan and green landscape photographs, accompanied by furniture designed by Northern European designers like Aalto and Tapiovvaara,

transport customers into a meditative and tranquil sanctuary from urban life. This Osaka coffee shop also bears all the understated elegance that hand-rendered script can offer. The childlike handwriting on the walls gives it an innocent charm, complementing the café's motive, which is to wish customers a good day with every cup of coffee.

The Scene of a Good Day

The Scene of a Good Day

The Scene of a G

Leckerbaer

Copenhagen, Denmark

ID & IN Re-public   **PH** Line Falck   **CL** Leckerbaer

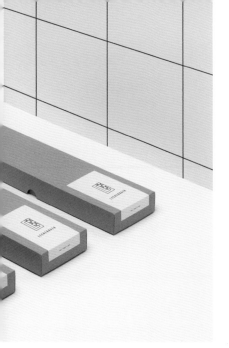

Run by two Michelin chefs, Leckerbaer in Copenhagen is famed for elevating the Danish butter cookie and other classic sweet treats to gourmet status. Re-public's visual identity for the bakery is dedicated to the form of cookie cutters and baking trays, creating an aesthetic that admires craftsmanship and culinary artistry. This concept is not only manifested in Leckerbaer's logo and packaging, but also in the consistently small, circular shapes of their pastries. The logo accentuates the letter 'L' using staggered geometric shapes, and altogether produces an impressive amalgam where classic patterns, a bold typeface and muted colours meet.

LECKERBAER

LECKERBAER

BAKING HOURS

TIRSDAG - FREDAG 10.00 - 18.30   LØRDAG 10.00 - 16.00   SØNDAG, MANDAG: L

Sorry Coffee Co.
Toronto, Canada

ID & IN Kit and Ace   **PH** Warren Michael Keefe   **PG** Ben Johnston   **CL** Kit and Ace

Located in both Toronto and London, Sorry Coffee Co. is a coffee bar initiated by renowned apparel brand Kit and Ace. Every three months, they collaborate with up-and-coming local artists and allow them to showcase their artworks on Sorry's signature blank canvas cups, effectively fueling a creative network through their coffee shop. Ben Johnston's art entry was made to resemble stamps, which give the cups a personalised, one-of-a-kind aesthetic. A sturdy, contemporary look is generated through bold, striped visuals. By playing with various aspects of design and typography, Sorry Coffee defies expectations of a normal café, allowing local creatives to feel cherished and at home.

SORRY

Revolver Coffee
Vancouver, Canada

ID Post Projects **IN** Ste Marie Design **PH** Grady Mitchell, Lucas Finlay **CL** Revolver Coffee

Revolver

BREW BAR • 325 CAMBIE STREET

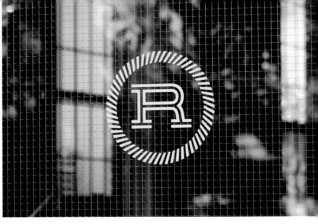

ESPRESSO BAR			BREW BAR		
Espresso	2⁷⁵		**Coffee**		Mrkt. Price
TWO FINGERS WORTH			SEE DAILY MENU		
Macchiato	3⁰⁰		**Tea**	3²⁵	
2 OZ ESPRESSO WITH A SPLASH OF TEXTURED MILK.			LOOSE LEAF BLACK, GREEN, OOLONG AND HERBAL.		
Cappuccino	3⁵⁰		**Tasting Flight**	9⁰⁰	
5½ OZ ESPRESSO AND TEXTURED MILK.			THREE COFFEES BREWED ONE WAY, 10-15 MIN.		
Latte	4⁰⁰		**Brew Flight**	9⁰⁰	
9½ OZ ESPRESSO AND TEXTURED MILK.			ONE COFFEE BREWED THREE WAYS, 10-15 MIN.		

Always striving to hone their craft, Revolver Coffee is a family-run coffee haunt in West Vancouver. Since Revolver places a heavy focus on the art of coffee-making, the café's identity made a revolving pattern its focal point, with swirls of strokes encircling a handsome and robust block letter 'R' that appears on its simple seasonal menu and windows. Inside the corner shop, an open laboratory-style brewing bar provides full transparency into the coffee tasting and brewing process. Three world maps created by thousands of nails echo Revolver's international influences, while steel fixtures and a menu made from wire mesh safety glass admire the elegant and historic block.

Coffee & Co.

Tallink Silja Line cruise

ID Bond Creative Agency   **CL** Tallink Silja Line

Situated on the Tallink Silja line cruise ship is a new cafeteria called Coffee & Co. that offers freshly made savoury and sweet snacks. Bond Creative Agency sought to create a friendly and straightforward environment through their branding that would cater to people of all ages. The logo uses a clever composition of typography to reveal a bird's eye view of a coffee cup, which simultaneously portrays the first two letters of the word 'coffee'. The use of a strict black-and-white palette in their collateral gives the café a solid and confident image that emulates their vision. The visually stimulating script typography gracefully dances along displays and packaging, embodying the friendly approach that they aimed for.

Good coffee goes a long way

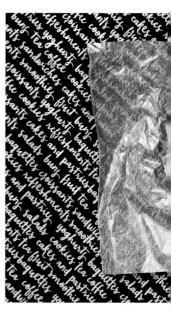

Stone Way Café

Seattle, USA

ID Shore   **IN** goCstudio   **CL** Stone Way Café

Seattle is home to the newly managed Stone Way Café, which was in need of a new brand identity that would better assimilate into the Fremont neighbourhood. Approaching the visuals with the area's industrial history in mind, Shore was inspired by the graphics and signage developed by tradesmen. With the help of local sign painters and fabricators, the store has developed a monogram with a simple typeface, the circular design of which evokes an essence of community spirit. With its enigmatic and dark exterior and warm wooden interior, Stone Way Café embraces Fremont's industrial past and the building's history of gentrification, as well as harnesses its own sense of identity and form of self-expression.

Dollop Coffee & Tea

Chicago, USA

ID & IN Firebelly Design   **CL** Dollop Coffee & Tea   **CR** Rightway Signs

EXPRESS
MENU

COFFEE				
COFFEE HOT	2	2.25	2.50
COLD BREW ICED	–	2.75	3
POUR OVER	–	3.50	–
LATTE/CAPP HOT / ICED	3.50	4	4.50
MOCHA HOT / ICED	4	4.50	5
MACCHIATO		3	
CORTADO			
AMERICANO HOT / ICED			

ALL PRICES INCLUDE TAX

| 2.50 ESPRESSO | SPECIALTY COFFEE DRINKS | 4 | 4.50 | 5 |

TEA				
CHAI TEA LATTE ICED ONLY MEDIUM OR LARGE	3.75	4.25	4.50
HOT TEA ONE SIZE	REGULAR 2.75	PREMIUM 3.50
ICED TEA HOT / ICED	–	2.75	3.50

BREAKFAST SERVICE —	
5/6 PIE SLICE	SANDWICHES SALADS SAVORY PIE PLATE QUICHE	8

| LUNCH SERVICE — | |

| SERVED ALL DAY | 5 YGRT PARFAIT | 2.50 VGN DONUT |

Sitting on the first floor of Chicago's Fisher Building is Dollop Coffee & Tea. A designated landmark designed by local architectural legend, Daniel Burnham, the building retains strict and rigorous rules of design. Thus, the designers at Firebelly Design worked to create an identity that would seamlessly immerse this café into all the historic art and architecture that surrounds it. The logo designs and logotypes feature heavy strokes that mirror Chicago's elevated train tracks, and are also designed to complement the building's glazed terracotta structure and detailed carvings. Since gold leaf hand lettering is currently a dying practice amongst shops and cafés, the designers decided to utilise this technique on window signage, achieving an authentic Chicagoan touch.

Voyageur du Temps

Los Altos, USA

ID & IN Character San Francisco · · · · · **PH** Todd Tankersley · · · · · **CL** Voyageur du Temps

Voyageur du Temps, meaning 'traveler of time', is an artisan bakery and café that lies in an area where a train station used to be. Inspired by the Roman numeral five from an old French clock in a train station, their logo exemplifies both the café's unique theme and location. For a place that fosters the idea of travelling through time, Character San Francisco manages to render their graphic identity and overall atmosphere so that it exudes a quality of timelessness. Their signature 'V' logo retains a thin hairline on one side, along with a much stockier opposing stroke on the other and a large full-stop that altogether exerts an authoritative air. Combined with the café's serious black and dark grey palette, this image conclusively brings together the brand's classic and uncompromising identity.

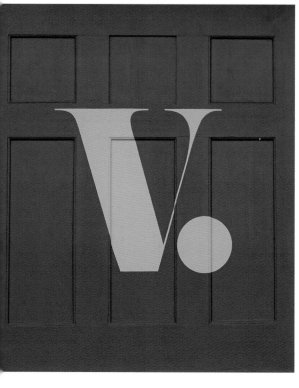

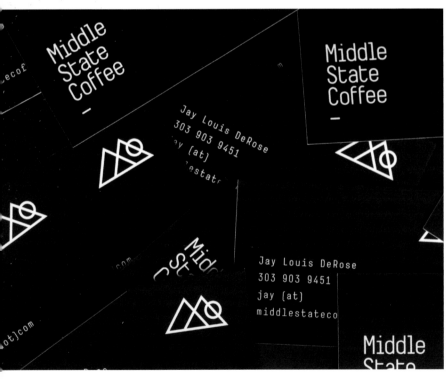

MiddleState Coffee

Denver, USA

ID Studio Mast   **CL** MiddleState Coffee

In the backroom of a men's clothing store in Denver, Colorado, known for its geographic diversity, Dustin Pace and Jay DeRose established a coffee bar that sought to reflect the area's true culture and spirit built around the mountains. Keen to deviate from patterns, motifs and colours commonly associated with the rocky terrain, the pair worked together with Studio Mast and developed a minimalist black-and-white logo featuring two mountains and a setting sun, all reduced to three simple, overlapping shapes. This visual summary, along with MiddleState Coffee's clean and crisp typewriter font, serves to tell how Coloradans easily delight in climbing rocks, hiking and skiing in the ranges.

Coffee Shops

—

Most of us have spent a fair share of time inside a coffee shop or two. Be it one of many global chains or a small independent café, they are like extended living rooms, mobile offices, hideaways and go to destinations while traveling. We could not imagine a world without them.

But as is the case with most other industries, coffee shops also greatly vary across the board from service to design and from quality to location. What then makes the perfect coffee shop?

For starters, a coffee shop has to be a welcoming place that makes you feel at home. It has to give you the feeling that you can spend hours on end there, whiling the day away over an expertly prepared cup of coffee and a delicious slice of something sweet. It has to be the place where you can learn something about coffee, instead of merely consuming it.

In certain cases, coffee shops have turned the art of making and serving coffee into something so exquisite that you forget what you came there for in the first place. In many of the world's most outstanding coffee shops, more attention is now being paid to the alternative brew methods that most of us regard as the purest form of brewing coffee. And this takes time, hence the name 'slow coffee'.

In certain parts of the world, like New York City or Scandinavia, filter coffee plays an important role, often edging out espresso sales. Would you consider standing in line for 20 minutes to get your morning filter coffee at your favourite coffee bar? What was unthinkable a few years ago is now becoming a reality in many places, such as New York City.

Ultimately, the coffee shop is the place where the fate of even the most expertly roasted coffee is at the hands of the barista. A good barista can turn your coffee into something truly magical, and a bad one can turn your coffee into an experience you would rather forget.

List of some spectacular coffee shops

About life coffee brewers, Tokyo | Alma Negra, Mexico City | La Fontaine de Belleville, Paris
Neo Coffee Bar, Toronto | Pascal, Stockholm | Roberto Café, Tehran | The Attendant, London
Truth Coffee, Cape Town

Photo courtesy of Verve Coffee Roasters

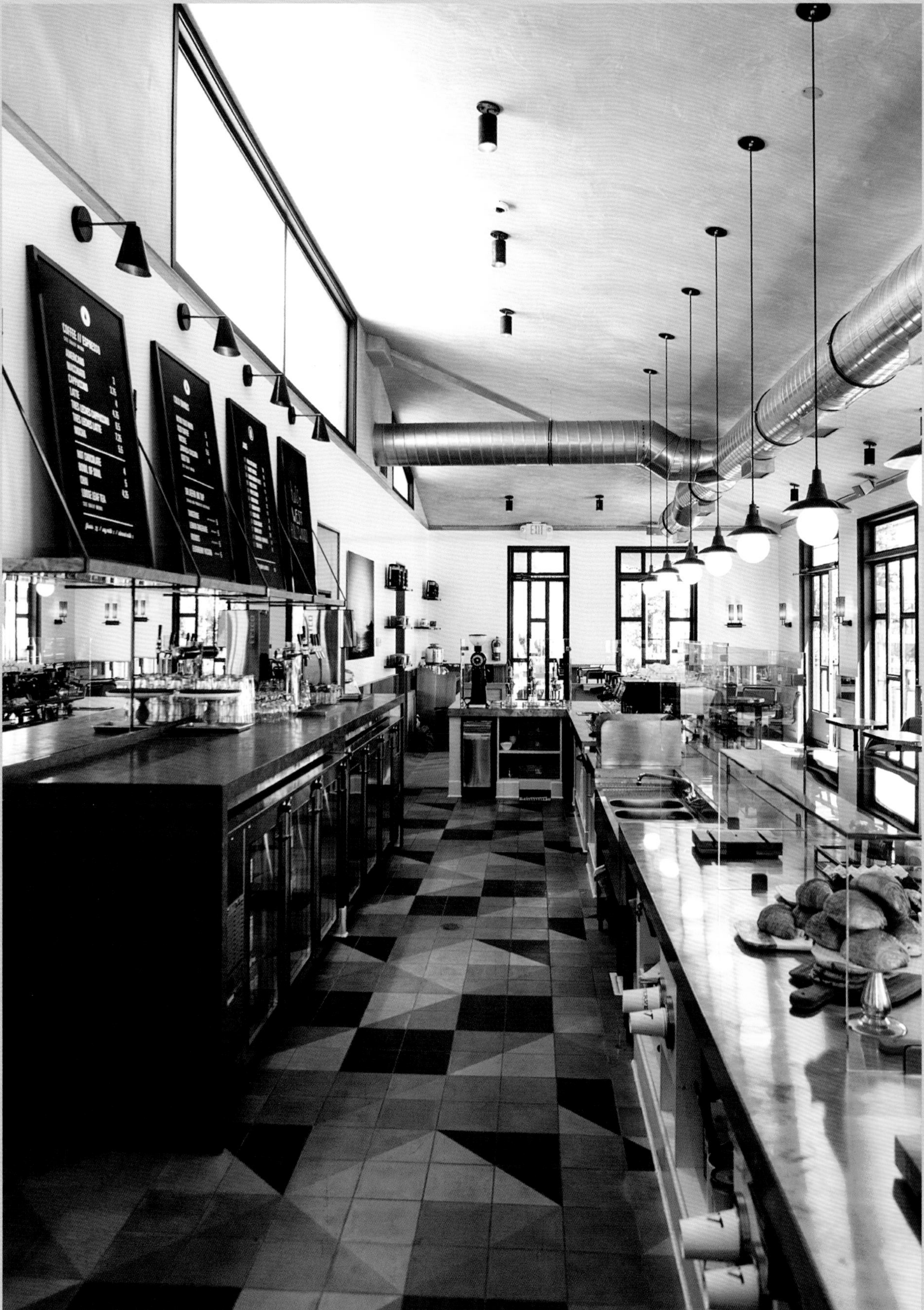

Hotel Daniel Bakery

Vienna, Austria

ID moodley brand identity   **IN** Atlier Heiss Architekten, Florian Weitzer   **CL** Weitzer Hotels Betriebsgesellschaft m.b.H.

Situated within Vienna's Hotel Daniel, the Daniel Bakery has become an urban hub for locals and tourists alike. Hotel Daniel brands itself as a place of "Smart Luxury", which emphasises the need for a flexible and light-hearted lifestyle for the modern traveller. Designed by Moodley, Daniel's visual identity mirrors the minimalism and high quality of contemporary design, while maintaining personal touch and a sense of heritage. Their logo features a faintly textured stamp print, a hallmark of the brand's confident and genuine approach. For Daniel Bakery, Moodley simply balanced the hotel's black-and-white logo with a fresh red colour scheme, effectually contradicting the hotel's luxurious and minimalist atmosphere with something more vibrant and boho-chic.

Be optimistic 😊 for the world.

HOTEL EST. 1886

URBAN STAY
DANIEL
SMART LUXURY

So schmeckt die Steiermark...

Fresh Ideas.

Coffee & Kitchen

Graz, Austria

ID moodley brand identity   **IN** Markus Kovac, Helmuth Fritz, Hannes Ziehrer   **CL** Coffee & Kitchen

Situated in the middle of a business district in Graz, Austria, Coffee and Kitchen strives to establish itself as an oasis dissociated with the formality and rigidity of the commercial world. A reinvention of the corporate coffee shop, Moodley created a black-and-white visual identity that mutes and contradicts the colour of the outside world. Accompanied by natural browns in parts of the interior and collateral design and an informal handwriting font in the logo, the brand's overall identity evokes a tranquility that is scarce amongst the usual urban buzz. Printing brand materials were consciously avoided, with the exception of logo stickers which are pasted onto cups, bags and stationery.

Keisari Bakery

Helsinki, Finland

ID Werklig   **IN** (Façade) Werklig, (Interior) Keisari Bakery / Pistrina Ltd   **CL** Keisari Bakery

In an attempt to renew their visual identity, Keisari Bakery has asked Weklig to help develop a new image that would communicate their wide range of products. With simplicity in mind, Werklig produced a black and white pattern similar to the scoring marks found in baked bread that could be easily adapted for use on various surfaces in converted colours. This strong and limited colour scheme contrasts with the colourful palette of the baked goods and also distinguishes from many other bakeries that tend to use natural browns in their identity. Ultimately, the aim was to highlight the warm colours and patterns found in the bakery's products through simple but effective design.

Vete-Katten

Stockholm, Sweden

ID The Studio   **IN** Millimeter Arkitekter   **PH** (Collateral) Susanna Blåvarg, (Space) Patrik Lindell   **CL** Vete-Katten

Vete-Katten has been serving artisan pastries and chocolates since 1928, rightfully earning its place as one of Stockholm's quintessential confectioneries. Tasked with constructing a new image for this well-loved institution, The Studio focused on rejuvenating and modernising the brand while maintaining its distinct Old-World charm. In contrast with the soft logotype preserved from their old identity, the Neutraface typeface used for all other typography offers a strikingly contemporary yet nostalgic expression. Along with the authentic off-white metal enamel signs, menu boards, the brand's new minimal aesthetic serves to accent the intricate craft and colour of their beloved pastries. The Studio beautifully captures the balance between Vete-Katten's playful personality and the spirit of old Swedish café culture.

FRUKOST
LUNCH
AFTERNOON TEA
BUTIK
BAKVERK
BRÖD
PRALINER

KONDITORI VETE-KATTEN
KUNGSGATAN 55 STOCKHOLM
ETABLERAT 1928

Yardstick Coffee

Makati, Philippines

ID ACRE   **PH** Jovian Lim   **CL** Yardstick Coffee

Intent on distinguishing itself from the many other coffee shop chains around the city, Yardstick Coffee offers a studio space in Philippine city, Makati, that accommodates a café, coffee roastery and coffee lab. Inspired by the desire to spread knowledge about specialty coffee around the Philippines, their logo resembles the national flag, rotated. Its open, minimalist design and use of diffused lights enhance the navigability of their studio space, producing an honest atmosphere where employees and customers can interact comfortably and freely. ACRE's functional aesthetics are wholly incorporated into Yardstick Coffee's interior, where simplistic wooden furnitures are accented with splashes of colour to add playfulness and vivacity to the shop's setting.

COFFEE

...ACK	120
...HITE	140
...AILY BREW	100
...AND BREW	160
...-HOUR COLD BREW	160
...OLD BREW W/ MILK	160

COFFEE CATALOG

LEGAZPI

PARADIGM

PROJECT Y

CONCEPT COFFEE

...EAR FRED,	190
...ON-DAIRY LATTE	150
...ANTA'S ICED WHITE	170
... TAKES TWO	300

PAIRINGS

Waffle !!!

+ Caramelized mango yogurt

+ Toasted almonds
+ Coconut shavings
w/ Chocolate drizzle
—120

BITES

SWEET
☑ ORANGE BLOSSOM BUTTER —110
☑ TOMATO JAM —140
w/ KESONG PUTI

SAVORY
☑ SARDINE CREAMCHEESE —120
☑ DEVILED EGGS w/ AVOCADO —140

NON-COFFEE

HOT CHOCOLATE	140
TEA	140
12-HOUR COLD BREW TEA	160
GS/3	338,000
PREMIUM PLUS	98,000

YARDSTICKCOFFEE.COM

BLACK & WHITE COFFEES ARE
DOUBLE SHOTS BY DEFAULT.

The Flour Pot Bakery

Brighton, UK

ID filthymedia   **IN** The Flour Pot Bakery   **PH** James French   **CL** The Flour Pot Bakery

With two popular stores under their belt, The Flour Pot Bakery is an iconic coffee shop situated within the bustling city of Brighton. Characterised by a muted palette, the bakery embraces a refreshingly simple and economic brand identity. Their logo, which features a rolling pin and spoon inside a flower pot, plays along with the pun in 'Flour Pot Bakery', and insinuates that the bakery essentially grows and breeds culinary excellence. In the interior space, the juxtaposition of their mainly white and dark grey palette with bread-orange brick walls introduces the bakery's seriousness towards maintaining high-quality food, as well as its dedication to nurturing a casual and cosy atmosphere.

OPEN

MONDAY
8:00AM – 7:00PM

TUESDAY
8:00AM – 7:00PM

WEDNESDAY
8:00AM – 7:00PM

THURSDAY
8:00AM – 7:00PM

FRIDAY
8:00AM – 7:00PM

SATURDAY
8:00AM – 7:00PM

SUNDAY
9:00AM – 6:00PM

BREAD

THE FLOUR POT

£1.75

Plain

THE·FLOUR·POT
BAKERY

THE·FLOUR·POT
LOYALTY CARD

THEFLOURPOT.CO.UK

THE·FLOUR·POT
BAKERY

BREAD

CLASSIC WHITE SOURDOUCH £1.60 / £3.00

ROWN SOURDOUGH

MADE · IN · BRIGHTON

b & b

Singapore, Singapore

Abbreviated from Bread&Biscuit, b & b is an experimental brand in Singapore looking to tell a narrative with its use of deconstructed illustrations and freeform typography. Their identity consists mainly of illustrations of nostalgic hybrid creatures, who hesitantly travel into metaphorical and foreign lands, and are interpreted by the viewers. By fusing reality and imagination, Oddds plays with our perceptions and sense of tangibility. With a palette of navy blues and tan browns, these quirky illustrations maintain a subtlety and intriguing energy that compels customers to inquire more into the narrative of the characters. These illustrations, paired with a generously spaced custom typeface, combine to portray an old-world fairy-tale that bathes in whimsicality and peculiarity.

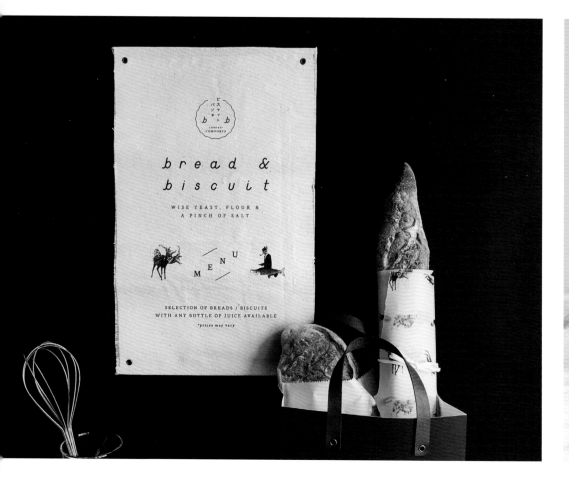

Cafe Decada

Prague, Czech Republic

ID Petr Kudláček / Lilkudley   **CL** Cafe Decada

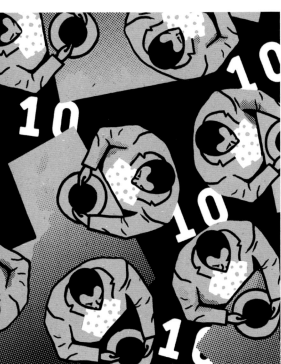

Café Decada sits on the historic location of Libeň, where workers from Prague used to live. It is also in close proximity to an old and abandoned railway track. Heavily inspired by Liben's history, the café's black-and-white visual identity features historical photographs of the town, coffee plants and a signature graphic of the globe. Lilkudley uses the globe graphic to symbolise the biggest cultural centre of Libeň at the turn of the century. These visuals possess the pleasant touch of manually screen-printed ink on 1.5mm recycled cardboard, and drink menus bound by hand with tape and screws.

Matamata

Paris, France

ID & IN Content Design Lab **PH** The White Shack Photography
SE (Environmental typography) Studio 6 Lettres **CL** Matamata

Hey!
There's more
ROOM
downstairs

Named after the rural New Zealand town where the Lord of the Rings trilogy was filmed, Matamata is a Parisian coffee bar run by two former Matamata residents. Coherently patterned in shades of green, Matamata's collateral and interior feature an explosion of exotic plants, oozing a much needed sense of warmth to break the daily grind. To accent the bar's casual vibe, Content Design Lab had Studio 6 Lettres paint Matamata's chalkboard signs, windows and directional cues in three dynamically distinct styles. Where robust inline typefaces, cursive writings and hand-drawn block letters set apart the owners' creed, menu offerings and other textual applications, the elegant single-lined logotype delicately summarises the owners' perfectionist approach to coffee and food.

Belle Epoque

London, UK

ID Mind Design   **IN** Belle Epoque Patisserie Ltd., Mind Design   **PH** Metz+Racine, Ed Reeve   **CL** Belle Epoque Patisserie Ltd.

Born out of owners Eric and Hulya Rousseau's extensive travel experiences, this French patisserie and boulangerie on London's Upper Street offers some of the city's finest desserts. Their signature motif features black-and-white eddies — a style reminiscent of Aubrey Beardsley's black ink drawings. As pattern is the main focus of their identity, the typography

used is relatively simple, and nicely juxtaposes the 60s' Hippie movement with Beardsley's Art Nouveau style. Mind Design additionally incorporated gold into the monotonous palette, the overall print design serving to draw attention to the colour and artistry of their pastries. Ultimately, Belle Epoque harmonises the grandeur of fine art and fine foods, achieving an identity that bathes in luxury and authenticity.

Tostado Café Club

Buenos Aires, Argentina

ID The brandbean   **IN** Hitzig Militello Arquitectos   **PH** Federico Kulekdjian, Cecilia Kelly, Buppa   **CL** Tostado Café Club

A reinvention of the classic 'tostado porteño', Tostado Café Club prides itself in its provision of fresh ingredients and high-quality coffee. The Brandbean designed everything from interior, packaging and signage, to dishware, uniforms and seat upholstery. The palette remains restricted to black-and-white, so that any application of colour can be used to indicate flavours. Hand-crafted icons were designed and printed on windows and walls, depicting various kitchenware and foods that can be found in the coffee shop. Camp-style cups, glazed facade plates, rustic interior and simple, readable typography offer a handsome atmosphere that is reminiscent of an old warehouse.

OFF-GRID CAFÉ
Physical
Hokkaido, Japan

ID COMMUNE   **IN** mangekyo   **SE** (Destruction) Monoi Komuten, Kenjiro Kobayashi, (Mural) Norihisa Hasega-
wa, (Plants) Flower Little, (Signage) Makers Base   **MT** Kitchen Nest   **CL** OFF-GRID CAFÉ Physical

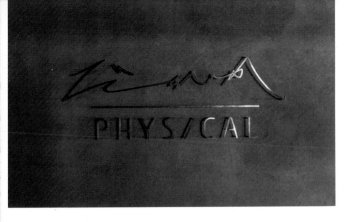

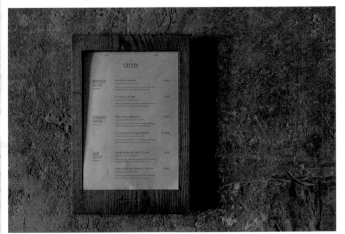

Situated in an off-grid location in Hokkaido, Japan, Physical Café thoroughly explores the experience of eating, feeling and living through unusual lens. Fixated on the idea of exposing the physical and elemental, COMMUNE plays with tactile senses by reducing properties of design to the utmost core, leaving behind raw surfaces, naturally dull and colourless palettes and factory-

style interior. Decorated with low-hanging industrial pendant lights, unvarnished wooden furniture and remnants of dead animals and trees, COMMUNE crucially exposes the habitually concealed natures of construction and deconstruction. PHYSICAL's double identity as café and dive bar further adds to its inherent novelty, profoundly defeating touchstones of an everyday coffee shop experience.

Cafe Diego

Abu Dhabi, United Arab Emirates

ID Backbone Branding   **IN** Redesign Gulf   **CL** Allied Brothers CO.

With its brand identity centering around the famed Argentine footballer Diego Armando Maradona, Café Diego's goal was to create a little piece of Argentina in Abu Dhabi. Visual cues around the restaurant see motifs such as "1986", suggesting the year when Maradona scored the "goal of the century", and iconic blue and white stripes derived from Argentina's national football jersey. Simultaneously influenced by Argentinian street art, the café space is infused with bold graphics, a psychedelic palette and stenciled designs, overall embodying a visual tribute to some of the best things that this spirited city has to offer.

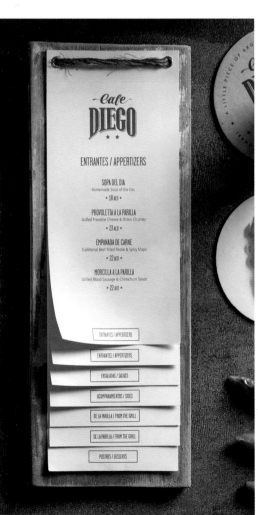

Cafe DIEGO

ENTRANTES / APPERTIZERS

SOPA DEL DIA
Homemade Soup of the Day.
• 18 AED •

PROVOLETTA A LA PARILLA
Grilled Provolone Cheese & Onion Chutney
• 23 AED •

EMPANADA DE CARNE
Traditional Beef Filled Pastie & Spicy Mayo
• 22 AED •

MORCILLA A LA PARILLA
Grilled Blood Sausage & Chimichurri Sauce
• 22 AED •

ENTRANTES / APPERTIZERS

ENTRANTES / APPERTIZERS

ENSALADAS / SALADS

ACOMPAÑAMIENTOS / SIDES

DE LA PARILLA / FROM THE GRILL

DE LA PARILLA / FROM THE GRILL

POSTRES / DESSERTS

Monjo Coffee

Kuala Lumpur, Malaysia

ID & IN Rice Creative   **CL** Monjo Coffee

New Malaysian coffee franchise Monjo Coffee is set to offer more than just a quick convenience. By comparing it to classic metro stations, Rice imagined a 'perfect Monjo station' where a traditional newsstand, a sandwich shop and a quality coffee point would roll into one. Taking cues from metro stations' wayfinding system designs, clear and easy-to-read block typefaces dominate their overhead menu and objects found around the shop are rendered into icons to adorn their cups. The theme continues on the heavy use of tiles inside and out, and their train-ticket-inspired loyalty cards, whimsically named as "personal pass", and café staff named "station managers".

ON J
· COFFEE ·

ESPRESSO	EXTRACTION OF 100% PURE ARABICA BEANS			
		S	M	L
CAPPUCCINO				
CAFFÈ LATTE		8.60	9.60	10.60
⊕ FLAVOR CARAMEL / HAZELNUT / VANILLA / CHOCOLATE		8.60	9.60	10.60
		10.10	11.10	12.10
CAFFÈ MOCHA				
		9.60	10.60	11.60
CARAMEL MACCHIATO				
		10.60	11.60	12.60
AMERICANO		7.60	8.60	9.60
ESPRESSO		6.60	7.60	

ICED COFFEE

ICED CAPPUCCINO

ICED LATTE
⊕ FLAVOR
CARAMEL / HAZELNUT / VANILLA / CHOCOLATE

ICED MOCHA

ICED CARAMEL MACCHIATO

ICED AMERICANO

OKTOKKI The Café

Seoul, South Korea

ID Onasup & Anzi   **IN** UZU   **CL** OKTOKKI The Café

OKTOKKI is a modern café in Seoul that puts a fusion twist on traditional Korean foods. This well-being café preserves its oriental image through the narrative of Korean fairytale, 'Oktokki', that revolves around a rabbit living on the moon. Inspired by this powerful mythical image, their visual identity features a series of iconic circular graphics, used to illustrate what the café offers. These monochromatic, minimally-designed icons symbolise various dishes and metaphors, such as 'super salads' or 'Ssaam and Baan' (Korean tapas). By mimicking the style of universal symbols that we all instantly recognise, Onasup and Anzi create a clever and playful identity for OKTOKKI that is familiar yet intriguing.

Ritaru Coffee

Hokkaido, Japan

ID COMMUNE   **PH** Kei Furuse   **WB** Imaginary Stroke

PT Manami Sato, Atsuhiro Kondo   **CP** Takashi Toi   **CL** Ritaru Coffee

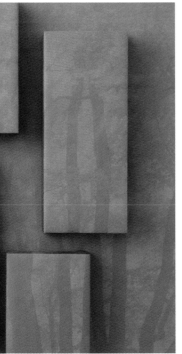

Ritaru Coffee's visual symbol is that of a tree-ring, which represents 'time', in particular the time and effort it takes to roast, serve and enjoy coffee. The coffee shop's interior, collateral design and even desserts are all influenced by patterns found on trees, instilling a constant reminder of the value of time and consequently encouraging customers to savour the carefully home-brewed coffees before them. The pervasiveness of wood-like products brings an appreciation of materiality and earthliness to the coffee shop's flavour. Along with the silent and speculative moonlit setting of the café, COMMUNE manages to achieve a brand identity which values coffee-making as an art form.

Cafés are a great place to unwind and pass the time while escorted by a mug of coffee or a delectable pastry. Whether decoration is opulent or minimal, vibrant or monotonous, each café's interior design sculpts an idiosyncratic world that articulates its own style and personality. By constructing functional and captivating spaces that will engender strong first impressions, customers not only become addicted to the coffee but also to the charming backdrops in which they enjoy it.

Interiors & Architecture

Visualising brand in space

The Penny Drop

Melbourne, Australia

ID Pop & Pac   **IN** We Are Huntly   **PH** (Collateral) Mark Lobo, (Space) Brooke Holm
CL The Penny Drop, Steven Liu and Mary Lai   **CR** S&K Group

East of Melbourne's central business district lies The Penny Drop, an all-day eatery where east meets west in both menu and decor. Playing with the concept of "penny dropping" from the pockets of the new Australian Tax Office above it, the restaurant shuns the boring corporate coffee shop image and embodies a circular theme throughout the space. Spherical lighting fixtures, round mirrors and a large curved bar all come together as a direct response to this idea, reinforced by a penny-inspired palette and copper materials, welcoming white collars and alike to come for a brief respite. The seating layout echoes the 'ripple effect' that the café wishes to have on its locale and residents of Box Hill.

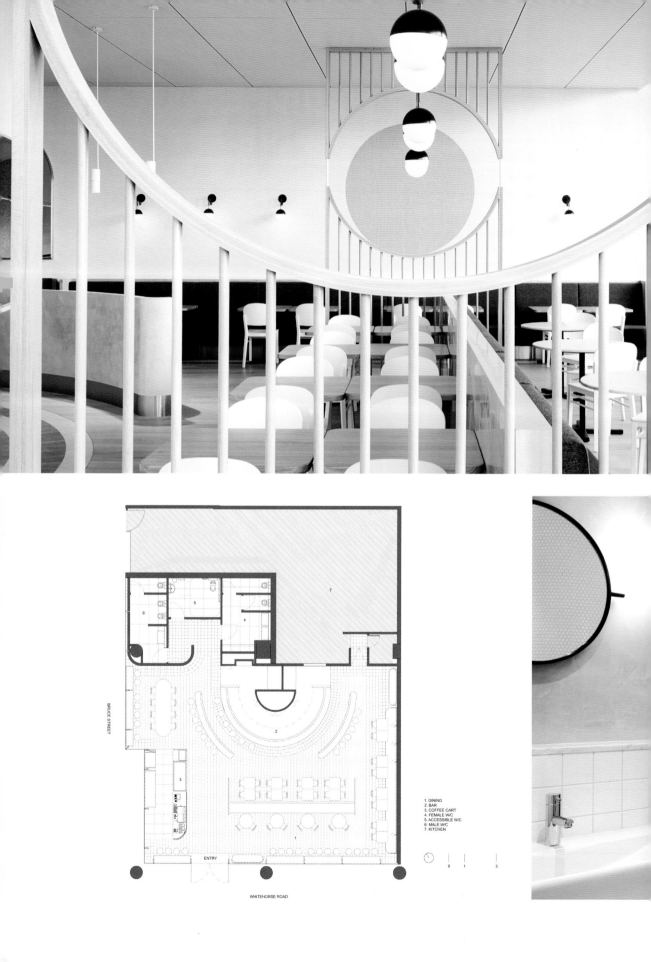

1. DINING
2. BAR
3. COFFEE CART
4. FEMALE W/C
5. ACCESSIBLE W/C
6. MALE W/C
7. KITCHEN

BRUCE STREET

ENTRY

WHITEHORSE ROAD

0   1   3

The Kettle Black Café

Melbourne, Australia

ID Pop & Pac   **IN** Studio You Me   **PH** Peter Clarke, Peter Firus   **CL** The Kettle Black Café

Located at the last heritage-listed site on Melbourne's Albert Street, The Kettle Black Café couples contemporary with classic styles. From the historic hexagonal floor tiles to water-stained white stone wash basins, the café draws from classical architectural elements to create a timeless look. Brass finishes and matte black steel accessories strongly contrast with the warm palette of soft oak, adding sleek touches of modern opulence to the space. To weave organic and playful accents into the aesthetic, potted plants, green chairs and organic linens are placed against the minimalist backdrop, elevating the novelty of such commonplace items.

THE
KETTLE
BLACK.

Bistro Proti Proudu

Prague, Czech Republic

IN Mimosa Architekti, Modulora   **PH** BoysPlayNice   **CL** Karolina Konečná, David Konečný

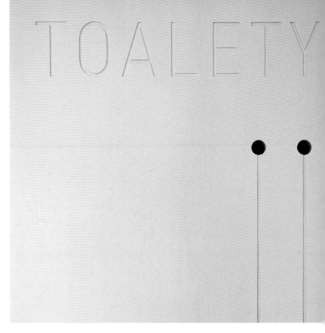
TOALETY

Inspired by locally born electrical engineer František Křižík, Prague-based eatery Bistro Proti Proudu integrates the themes of current and connection into their interior design. Made of perforated plywood, the main bar wall displays black cables that embody grid-like patterns on a white surface. Forming a network of wires stretching from switches behind the counter to pendant light fixtures suspended above tables, this central motif personifies a tangible connection between staff and customers. The use of motion detector lighting, which turns on and off as customers enter and exit through the main door, also enhances the tangency between guests and the coffee shop's energy. Soft plywood textures echo with the stone floor pattern elegantly, contrasting with the black steel accents on lights and chairs.

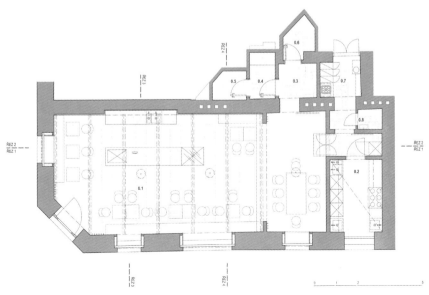

Café Ferdinand

Hamburg, Germany

ID & IN Aerogram Studio   **PH** (Collateral) Kyle Born, (Space) Christian Köster   **CL** Vodafone

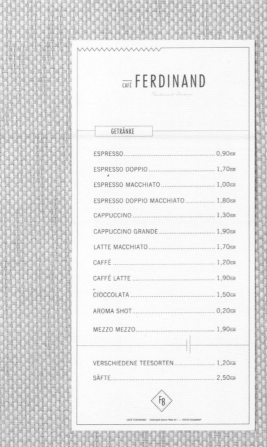

Inspired by Nobel Prize winner Karl Ferdinand Braun, Café Ferdinand is a nod to the German inventor's significant contribution to modern telecommunications. Integrating elements of Bauhaus design, a style prominent in Braun's time, the café features a display of retro-looking curios that resonate with Braun's inventions, such as an impressive collection of vintage telephones. As an ode to his work as a professor, as well as to the import of scholarship, the space is designed to resemble a classroom, shown by blackboard drawings and study desks with cubby holes underneath. Full of books and period details, the elevated library area is perfect for exchanging intellectual thoughts and conceiving new creations.

Open 10:00–19:50

FERDINAND

Probieren Sie
Omas Handgefilterten
Kaffee mit einem
Stück

ODIN Café + Bar

Toronto, Canada

ID Bandito Design Co   **IN** Phaedrus Studio   **PH** Ryan Fung   **SE** (Mural) Tara Rose
CL Odin Café + Bar, Thor Espresso Bar

ODIN Café and Bar is situated in downtown Toronto, within a neighbourhood that fosters increasingly demanding standards of architecture and design. It embraces a sophisticated industrial aesthetic in the form of a concrete box lined with expansive glass walls. Structural columns intercept the café's middle, naturally distinguishing the front-of-house's crowded bars from the more casual low-table seating at the back. The vision for this hybrid venue was to mimic a landscape of natural rocks and ice. These elements are translated into the modern setting through sculptural furnishings expressing various diagonal planes, retaining a glacial yet elegant quality. The touches of warm wood extending across the interior lining of ODIN's structure contrast the craggy facets with a warm and inviting flavour.

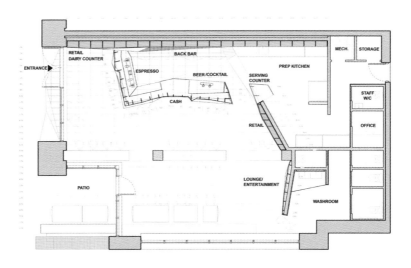

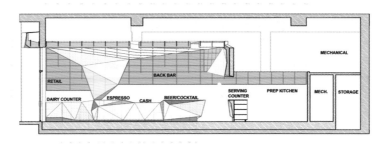

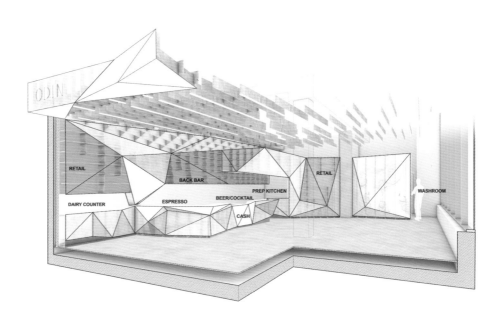

Mixed Retail Spaces

—

While it is no secret that many coffee roasters have begun to embrace fully equipped kitchens serving delicious foods all day long, or even a banging cocktail after hours, there are also a few other concepts that skillfully combine coffee with another category.

In some instances, we have even seen government institutions turn to independent coffee roasters to help spruce up their buildings, as was recently the case when the British Library invited Origin Coffee Roasters to set up shop inside its King's Cross location.

Across many cities, we have also seen incredible retail spaces opening up a part of their space to coffee bars that either operate independently or form part of the store's whole.

Although the idea of buying a cup of coffee in a bookstore is nothing new, it happens to be the more creative spaces that are reinventing the traditional retail space.

What a better way to browse for art, clothes, books or racing bikes while holding a delicious cup of coffee in your hand. What's more, many of these spaces occupy spectacular locations that would otherwise be out of budget for most coffee entrepreneurs.

List of some creative retail spaces that also serve coffee

Blacktop, Los Angeles | Coffee & Vinyl, Antwerp | Parlor Coffee @Persons of Interest, New York City
Petra, Istanbul | Rapha, London | Roots Coffee, Bangkok | Wer-haus, Barcelona | Westberlin, Berlin

Radosti Coffee

Saint Petersburg, Russia

ID Orka Collective   **IN** Asya Baranova, Nikolay Pokorsky   **PH** Asya Baranova
FT Verstak & Delo   **CL** Radosti Coffee

Living up to their name 'Radosti' (meaning 'joy' in Russian), this St. Petersburg-based coffee shop promotes healthy and happy living through all the senses. Not only does Radosti Coffee manifest its mission through the tastebuds, it also does so through the natural and refreshing qualities of its wood-clad, plant-infused interior. Coupled with high ceilings and large panoramic windows, these designs not only flood the interior with welcoming natural light, but also offer a sweeping view of the Neva river. This candid tangency between the natural and urban world serves to revitalise Radosti Coffee's desire to cultivate a beatific environment for their customers. Additionally, to accent the lush vegetation inhabiting the café space, bathrooms are painted a teal-green, the effervescent quality of which adds a refreshing tenor to the joyful coffee shop landscape.

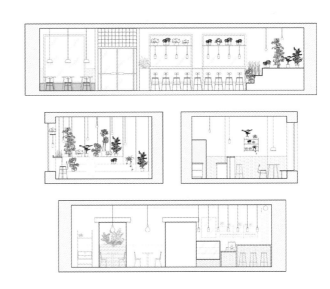

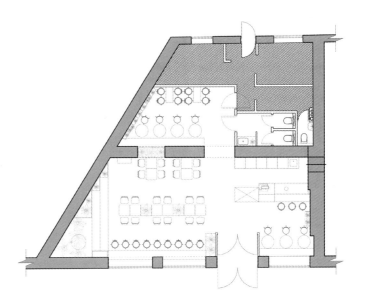

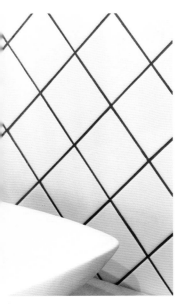

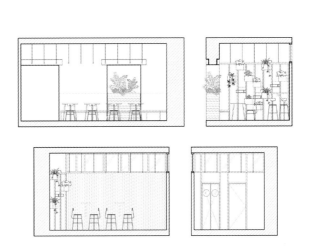

Barry Café

Melbourne, Australia

ID The Company You Keep (TCYK)   **IN** Technē Architecture + Interior Design
PH Ben Hosking   **CL** Barry Café

Techne Architecture and Interior Design renovated the Melbourne-based Barry Café by making simple yet consequential adjustments to reflect the neighbourhood's community-minded attitude. The original Victorian façade has been refitted with floor-to-ceiling steel frame windows, allowing for natural light and cool breezes to float through the interior, and bringing Barry Café in closer harmony with the streetscapes. Crucially, the original dark interior was stripped to make room for a much brighter colour scheme, manifested in the whitewashed brick walls and beige wood furniture. Pine shelves, in particular, are an example of Techne's simple yet functional approach. Wrapped along two sides of the room, the shelves provide necessary storage and a system of display that transcends versatility.

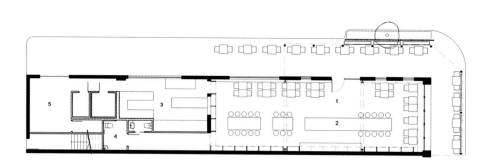

The Birds & The Beets

Vancouver, Canada

ID Post Projects   **IN** SUA   **TY** Alex Nelson, Ross Milne   **PH** Grady Mitchell   **CL** The Birds & The Beets

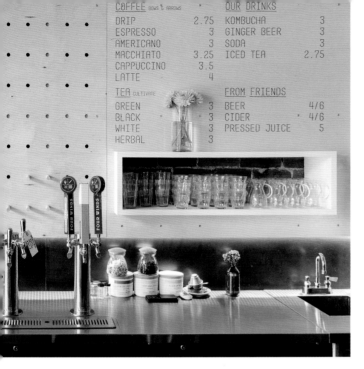

COFFEE BOWS & ARROWS		OUR DRINKS	
DRIP	2.75	KOMBUCHA	3
ESPRESSO	3	GINGER BEER	3
AMERICANO	3	SODA	3
MACCHIATO	3.25	ICED TEA	2.75
CAPPUCCINO	3.5		
LATTE	4		
TEA CULTIVATE		FROM FRIENDS	
GREEN	3	BEER	4/6
BLACK	3	CIDER	4/6
WHITE	3	PRESSED JUICE	5
HERBAL	3		

The Birds & The Beets is a café that welcomes its visitors with homemade comfort food and an atmospheric space, appropriate for an urban getaway. Boho-chic facets such as battered wood floors and exposed patinated masonry shape the vintage and historical vibe of the space, while the vibrant arrangement of greenery and knick-knacks renders a colourful and friendly homelike environment. Large panel windows infiltrated by plenty of sunlight offer the interior a cheery ambience, which accompanied with hand-painted signage, Baltic birch tables and hot rolled steel enhance the café's comfortable allure.

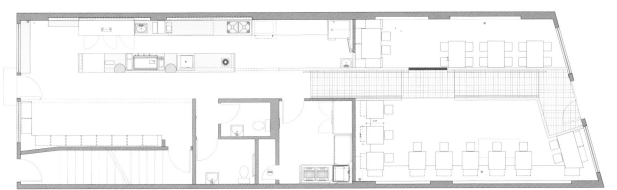

nest by AIA

Hanoi & Saigon, Vietnam

ID Giang Nguyen   **IN** The Lab Saigon   **CL** AIA Life Insurance

Designed by The Lab Saigon, nest by AIA is a financial loft and café that breeds connectivity and warmth. Located in two of Vietnam's most popular cities, nest Saigon serves as a relaxing retreat from the speed of the city, whereas nest Hanoi is inspired more by the natural landscapes of North Vietnam. Organic tones of light-coloured wood and greenery fill the interior space, nurturing a comfortable yet refined undercurrent. The open-plan setting of the loft accommodates an environment where people can interact and share knowledge, equipped with a number of round tables to foster a collaborative atmosphere. Large windows channel warm natural light into the interior, filling the space with an effervescent mood.

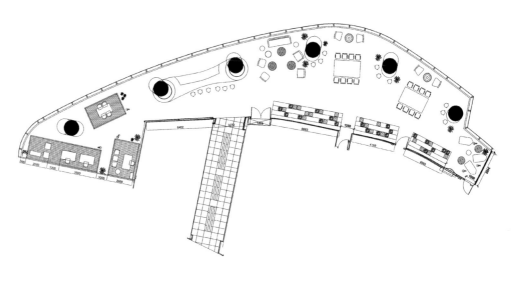

nest Saigon

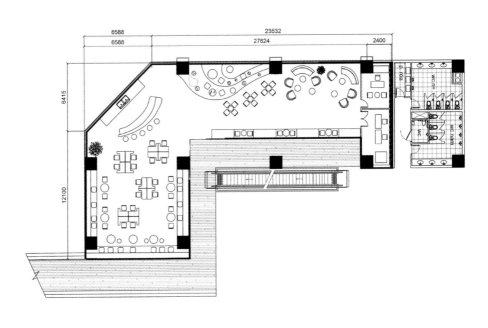

nest Hanoi

Other Coffee Concepts & Products

—

Until a few years ago, coffee was just coffee. It was something you drank to give you that energy boost to get you going in the mornings or something that grandma served to go with her cake on Sunday afternoon.

Yet, while coffee roasters and coffee bars have opened up a whole new world to us as coffee consumers, there are many other ways that you can experience coffee.

One very successful and effective way to discover truly amazing coffee is through coffee subscription services. Many coffee roasters offer their own mail order services that allow people to enjoy their freshly roasted coffees independent of where they are. However, there are also a handful of multi-roaster services like The Coffeevine, that people can subscribe to to receive a box full of carefully curated coffees from a myriad of different roasters.

And that's not all. Some coffee roasters and other independent beverage companies are producing bottled cold brew coffee that you can purchase at your local convenience store; craft beer brewers are teaming up with roasters to create coffee infused beers; some bakers like The Green Rabbit in Stockholm even use chaff, a byproduct of coffee roasting, in their pastries.

You can even get body scrubs made with ground coffee or buy 'grow your own mushroom' kits that use discarded coffee grounds as soil.

One thing we can certainly learn from this is that coffee is an incredibly diverse product that continues to have many uses even after you have brewed that perfect cup.

Some notable coffee concepts & coffee products

Monthly coffee box by The Coffeevine | Coffee subscription by Blue Bottle | Cold brew coffee by Stumptown | Coffee sour beer by Rare Barrel and Sightglass Coffee Roasters | Organic mushroom farm kit by Back to the Roots | Coffee scrub by Frank Body | Dark chocolate bar with Stumptown Coffee by Mast Brothers

Vitra x Blue Bottle Coffee
Special Exhibition
Tokyo, Japan

IN Schemata Architects   **PH** Koji Honda   **CL** Vitra

During Tokyo Design Week in 2015, Swiss furniture company Vitra collaborated with Schemata Architects to put on a temporary installation which featured the hallmarks of American café chain, Blue Bottle Coffee. Converted from a former storage building, this makeshift café carried a robust industrial image that was exemplified through exposed pipes along the ceilings and a plethora of metal furnishings. Contrasted by the elegant structure of Vitra's Belleville Chairs and Belleville Tables, the café's frosty atmosphere became refined with elements of aesthetic grandeur. Window panels wrapped around the building allowed for natural light to suffuse the interior, while also maintaining a transparency between neighbouring spaces, enabling a relationship between external and internal realms.

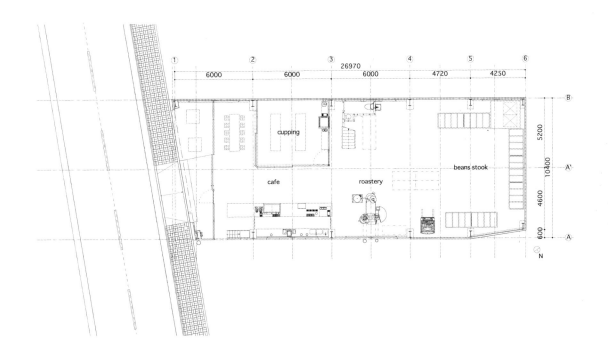

Ground floor café and roastery

Brawn & Brains Coffee

Geylang, Singapore

ID & IN Studio Juju **PH** Marc Tan **PG** Kinetic **CL** Brawn & Brains Coffee

Located in a former Singapore badminton hall, Brawn & Brains Coffee embraces its architectural roots and fashions it into a refreshing and modest café. A strong characteristic of the space is its ceiling structures which mould the underside of the hall gallery's bleachers above it. Adopting a utilitarian approach, Studio Juju highlights the authority of functional design and architecture to maximise space and comfort. This principle is reflected in the use of long refectory tables and compact stools, mirroring the style of a communal canteen. Pendant wire lamps suspended from the ceiling, steel counters and a mainly monotonous colour scheme combine to achieve a sleek industrial style. The overall use of neutral tones and weathered surfaces adds metallic touches to the space, while large windows allow the interior to drench in ample sunlight.

POPA~
YAN

BRAWN & BRAINS

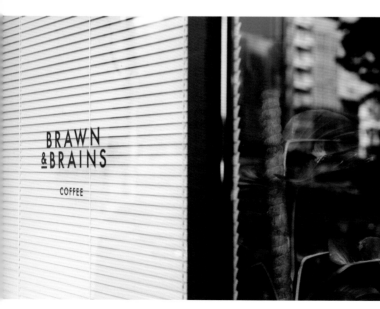

BRAWN
&BRAINS

COFFEE

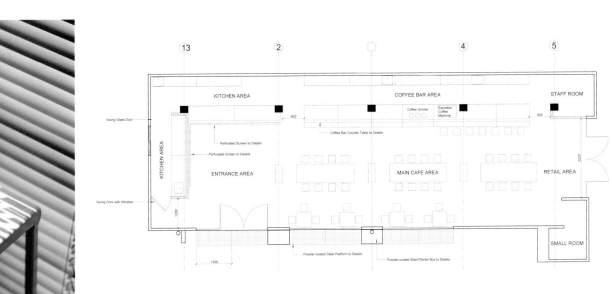

KITCHEN AREA

COFFEE BAR AREA

STAFF ROOM

Swing Glass Door

KITCHEN AREA

Perforated Screen to Details

Perforated Screen to Details

ENTRANCE AREA

Coffee Grinder

Espresso Coffee Machine

Coffee Bar Counter Table to Details

MAIN CAFE AREA

RETAIL AREA

Swing Door with Window

SMALL ROOM

Powder-coated Steel Platform to Details

Powder-coated Steel Planter Box to Details

PULP

Kuala Lumpur, Malaysia

ID Elita Ong   **IN** Elita Ong, Brandon Hng   **PH** Jovian Lim   **CL** Papa Palheta (M) Sdn Bhd

An offshoot of the Singaporean coffee company Papa Palheta, PULP has sparked a lot of buzz amongst coffee-lovers in Kuala Lumpur. Its name alludes to the pulp of coffee fruit and to the location's previous capacity as paper printing factory. By maintaining a warehouse exterior and repurposing an old guillotine paper cutter into a coffee table, PULP salvages and preserves old materials, attracting customers to take part in their functional yet charming aesthetic. The space within also features a number of mobile counters carrying coffee-making equipment, which enable customers to freely participate in brewing workshops. PULP is part café, education centre, workshop and showroom — altogether constructing a retail experience that fuels curiosity and educates customers about the peculiarities of coffee culture.

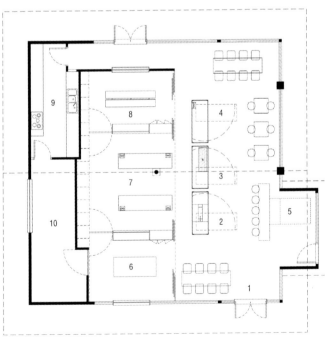

The Blue Cup
coffee shop
Kiev, Ukraine

ID Mixim Nazarov   **IN** Kleydesign   **PH** Anya Garienchik   **CL** The Blue Cup coffee shop

Popular among coffee gourmands in Ukraine, The Blue Cup coffee shop wanted an interior overhaul after expansion. Hoping to raise awareness of environmental conservation, Kleydesign and local artist Nastya Ptichek joined hands and brought to life a herd of the country's endangered species across the walls and furnishings, with sarcastic expressions revealing the reasons that led to their extinction. To take the edge off the solemn topic, vibrant colours and lighting fixtures brighten up the basement café while the wooden ceiling, tiles and textured wall add visual interest to a room with a limited view.

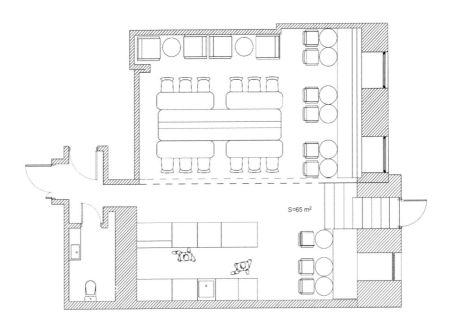

S=65 m²

Café L'étage

Kiev, Ukraine

ID Igor Libertarian   **IN** Kleydesign   **CL** Café L'étage

Located in the Ukrainian capital of Kiev, Café L'étage is a mono-cuisine restaurant decorated in eclectic styles. From flavourful tile designs and stained glass windows to artificial animal mounts, the space blends furnishings made in a multitude of striking materials and fabrics. Overhanging light bulbs of different sizes tastefully highlight the interior, boosting visual interest and enhancing the café's dynamism. A wealth of green plants not only adds to the jungle-like atmosphere of the space, but also accents the olive-coloured furniture, manifesting a profusion of visual echoes within the space. With lush satin curtains separating tables and a variety of seating to choose from, Café L'étage becomes a versatile space that accommodates for intimate and casual settings.

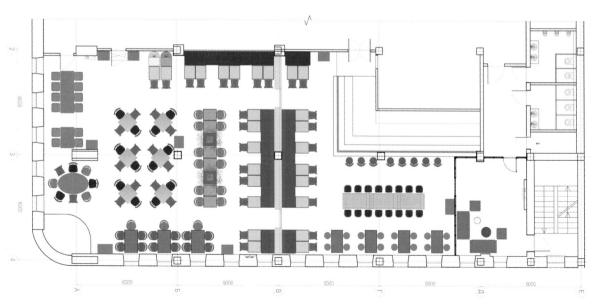

LAB O

Seoul, South Korea

ID McRoad & Co   **IN** studioVASE   **PH** Woo-Jin Park
FT studioVASE, IRO DESIGN+PLANNING   **ST** Seung-hui Kim   **CL** LAB O

LAB O is a Seoul-based dessert café known for being frequented by celebrities. With an aim to unify all human activity into one single space, LAB O integrates the baking lab into the main hall so that customers can relish in the art of baking pastries through large panoramic windows. To maximise efficiency, the space

consists of four kitchens in total: two for performance use and two for functional use. By featuring a range of spectacles to attract customers, the café fuels dynamic movements across the lab's space, fostering a stimulating and gregarious atmosphere. The space is also filled with furnishings reminiscent of American diners, but accented with shades of brown and maroon to add a touch of vintage to the overall picture.

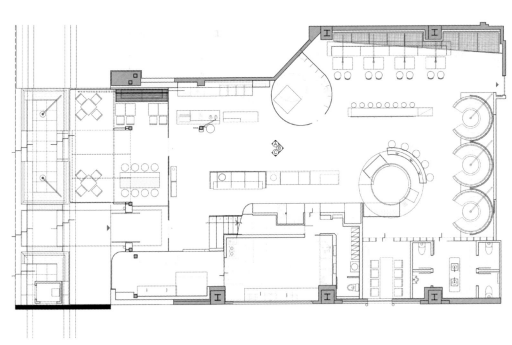

Don Café House
Coffee Shop

Pristina, Kosovo

ID & IN INNARCH   **PH** Atdhe Mulla   **CL** Don Café House L.L.C.

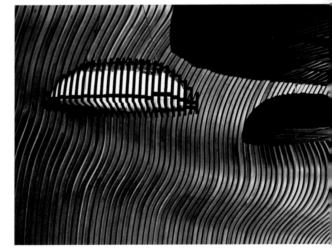

INNARCH conceptualised the interior of Don Café House to look like the inside of a burlap sack filled with coffee grains. Coloured in various shades of brown, the iconic wall made of plywood is arranged in a topographic fashion, functioning as seats and also offering a rhythmical aesthetic to the coffee shop's interior.

Likewise, the front wall behind the bar not only completes the shape of the bag, but also operates as a display shelf. Tables and hanging chandeliers shaped like coffee beans arranged around the space asymmetrically impersonate the space within a coffee sack. Complemented by soft and subdued lighting, the space glows with a warm and convivial air.

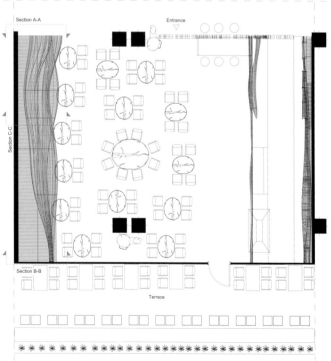

Section A-A

Entrance

Section C-C

Section B-B

Terrace

Shan Café

Beijing, China

IN Robot 3 Design   PH Xixun Deng   CL Shan Café

Named after the Chinese word for mountain, Shan Café has constructed an identity that recalls the imagery of the natural environment. A palette of earthy tones manifests itself in the form of wood, cardboard and brick furnishings, while the handmade pinewood wall mimics the firewood storage units in Chinese villages. The appealing exhibition of raw and natural materials also serve to reveal the workers' laborious efforts during construction, communicating its surviving vitality and spirit. Seeking to cultivate a functional space where customers feel encouraged to engage and interact, the café also incorporates a mezzanine which leads to an underground space. Not only does this maximise space, but it also gives customers the experience of 'walking into a mountain' as they enter the basement through a set of stairs.

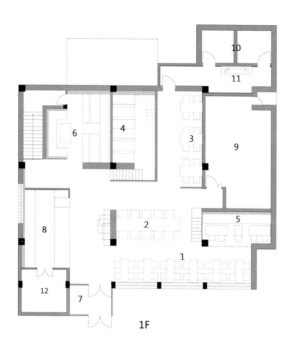

1F

Six Degrees

Jakarta, Indonesia

ID NOEEKO   **IN** OOZN   **PH** Irene Iskandar, Kanoo Studio   **CL** Six Degrees

Enveloping nearly the entire café interior, an undulating skin of timber slats turns Six Degree Café into a hallmark of cosiness within a mall in Jakarta. These layered fins of varying depth were crafted by local carpenters. Not only do they serve to break the monotony of spatial height over the 16-metre long shop front, but they also conceal ceiling equipment and improve the café's interior acoustics. Where warm timber and natural tones render a comfy environment, a polished concrete floor and generally cool black tone virtually offset the outside heat. Four types of seating create a meeting place for groups of different sizes to socialise over a good cup of java, which the café owner had envisioned from the very beginning.

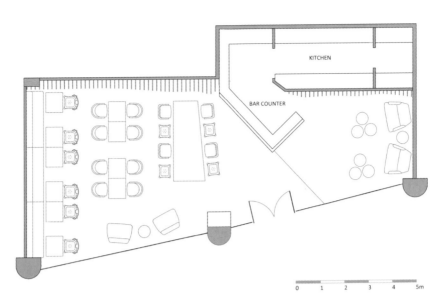

KITCHEN

BAR COUNTER

0 1 2 3 4 5m

EXPERT TALK

on brand applications and interiors

———

VISUAL IDENTITY

Sabine Kernbichler & Nicole Lugitsch, moodley brand identity
Antti Hinkula, Kokoro & Moi

INTERIOR BRANDING

Kylie Dorotic & Alicia McKimm, We Are Huntly
Yova Yager, Kleyvdesign

EXPERT TALK
ON VISUAL IDENTITY

————

moodley
brand identity

————

Dialogue with Art Directors
Sabine Kernbichler & Nicole Lugitsch

Award-winning design agency moodley brand identity has been developing corporate and product brands since 1999. Dedicated to discovering the origins and processes of cultivating coffee, moodley has always remained honest and true to the narratives behind their products. In harnessing the idea that branding has the power to communicate with people, they strive to conjure creative solutions which can both harmonise and inspire. moodley's strength is to derive clarity and truth from complex ideas, a trait which is manifested in their multidisciplinary and emotionally-appealing designs.

How would a well-executed brand identity reinforce coffee experience?

A well-executed coffee branding never equals soulless decoration. For all its style and positioning, there is always a good concept behind it. It helps patrons de-stress and conveys special feelings and values upon their first taste. In the best-case scenario, a good branding concept unites vision, packaging and the gastronomic experience in one harmonious picture.

What aspects of café branding would you consider most critical at present?

Good branding is not about following trends, but to create them. Rather than using trending vocabularies that have little to do with the product, it is important to use honest expressions to tell a true brand story. The subject of coffee in particular offers a wide range of topics around the coffee's origin, cultivation and the farmers. Here in Austria we also think of how trades are conducted.

What has moodley done to ensure continuity between Coffee & Kitchen's graphic identity and space?

NL: Branding and architecture went hand in hand to create a pleasant ambience that would communicate the fresh, honest and well-priced daily dishes, snacks and coffee that Coffee & Kitchen provides. I began with three mood boards concerning the decision to combine black-and-white with light wood in the interior. I found that even the haptic of the brown menu cards and packaging harmonised with the natural woods of the furniture.

Why do you think a typographic design works with Coffee & Kitchen in the first place?

NL: A typographic design works perfectly with Coffee & Kitchen because it is able to enhance the special values of the brand innovatively and at multiple touchpoints. Coffee & Kitchen is a day restaurant serving high quality, freshly handmade food in a business district — a "noble" culinary pleasure. Working extensively with stickers, we mainly use a playful handwriting font and illustrations to convey the image of a laid-back and pleasant atmosphere that is key to making the restaurant a favoured place. It is occasionally interrupted by a reduced straight typography, which presents the "noble" experience far away from any canteen-monotony or quick bite for in-between times. Typography is so to say the handwriting of the project and directs the tonality.

How different is your approach when it comes to devising a graphic identity as part of a larger one for Hotel Daniel Bakery?

SK: Hotel Daniel Bakery is lobby, restaurant and hotel shop all in one. Since it is the first thing you see upon entering the Daniel Vienna, you can imagine it is an important part of the hotel. You can enjoy good international cuisine from early till late, hold a business meeting or just chill out with friends at the loft style ground floor space here. This special laid-back atmosphere essentially epitomises what the entire hotel stands for. That's why it was very important to integrate the umbrella brand into the Bakery's branding without competing with it. In this case, the typography and logo were adapted from the hotel branding to make it recognisable as part of the establishment. But the fresh red colour distinguishes the bakery from the monochrome corporate design of the Daniel Vienna.

How do the elements in the identity correspond to the Hotel's motto of "Smart Luxury"?

SK: Smart Luxury (all you really need for good sleeping and good eating) stands for a reasonable price in a prime location in Vienna. The branding of the bakery is decorated with numerous fresh and winking details that embody on a small scale what the hotel stands for — urban, lively and reduced. For example, the yellow paper placemats that draw attention to the bee colonies located on the hotel rooftop and the upcycled food tags at the breakfast buffet.

The Mangolds logo uses a mix of bold typefaces, which revives the jovial atmosphere of the restaurant.
page 028

Logo stickers are passed onto cups, bags and stationery of Coffee & Kitchen.
page 116

The Daniel Bakery's logo features a faintly textured stamp print, a hallmark of the brand's confident and genuine approach.
page 110

"A well-executed coffee branding never equals soulless decoration. For all its style and positioning, there is always a good concept behind it. It helps patrons de-stress and conveys special feelings and values upon their first taste."

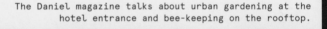

The Daniel magazine talks about urban gardening at the hotel entrance and bee-keeping on the rooftop.

The play on colours, fonts and typefaces is also prominent in Mangolds' interior.

What is it like to brand a café?

When refreshing a brand with rich heritage like Fazer, you have to decide if there are qualities to save and expand on, elements to introduce, and things to omit. You know it's done well if a new identity is fresh and inspiring without losing ties with the old one. Other than that, you need to understand what's happening around you and where the world is going. The designer should also focus on the end-user and create something meaningful and inspiring for him/her.

How can graphic identity help a café stand out within Helsinki's wealth of coffeehouses?

Here many new shops are established by the younger generation of entrepreneurs who are very passionate about what they do and have a good nose for current trends and aesthetics. That gives us a good chance to try more new things and create contemporary designs with a unique twist. Sadly many designers tend to play safe instead.

Is it true that Kokoro & Moi devises a new typeface for every project? Why?

When we started in 2001, we set some "rules" for our design process. One of which was to avoid repeating typefaces in our projects. It was not meant to be serious but somehow we kept to it. There came a point when the number of projects we were working on exceeded the number of designs released by foundries, so we started creating types in-house. So far I guess we've designed about 20 types. Type plays a big role in our work. You can definitely achieve something unique, strong and memorable with bespoke typefaces that no one else is using.

You say you play with what you can with no preconceptions. Is that an antidote to the current scene?

Our approach and attitude have always been playful and experimental. Design is one of the few areas where this kind of approach is possible. I think many designers are unaware of what opportunities they have in hand and produce work that looks just like everything else.

What were you trying to achieve when you renewed Fazer's brand?

Fazer is respected and well-known among the Finns. It has opened doors and led the way for the city's coffee scene. Fazer's logo and brand colour (blue) are iconic, so we wanted to retain those essential brand elements in the identity and refresh them by adding touches drawn from the history of the brand.

What led you to create Fazer Grotesk and Fazer Chisel?

In search for useful elements to refresh the brand's identity, we went through Fazer's archives and came across one thing that caught our eyes. That was the old Fazer signage at the entrance of their Kluuvikatu branch — the very first café opened by Karl Fazer. The type used in the signage had not been used anywhere else. Since it was unique and full of character, we decided to make this type a key element in the new identity. We also created patterns based on treasures we found from the archives.

How do Fazer's graphic identity and interior harmonise with each other?

We worked very closely with our interior design partner, Koko3. Their style and approach are as bold and playful as ours, so it was clear from the start that Fazer's graphic identity would play a key role in the café's interior. In the end, the typefaces, patterns and palette overwhelmed the surfaces and furniture in our new interior.

To what extent has Fazer's brand identity enhanced consumers' experiences?

The brand was already strong and popular but it has become even more attractive to Fazer's old and new customers since the renewal. Our work was not only about redesigning Fazer's identity but also rethinking Fazer's concept and services. One critical part of our job was to craft a journey for the customers which would better respond to present and future requirements about good coffee shop experience.

Founded in 2010, Helsinki-based creative agency Kokoro & Moi is always seeking for ways to set new standards and build progressive and bold concepts. With a fresh perspective on the world, the team has developed a strong focus on strategy, identity and design, making a mark on creative media. A belief in the power of design to transform brands and interrogate norms, their ideas constantly evolve and play with social pretensions — a mindset with no limits to the imagination. Kokoro & Moi has worked with a broad range of commercial players, from multinationals and start-ups to cultural and public institutions.

**EXPERT TALK
ON VISUAL IDENTITY**

———

Kokoro & Moi

———

Dialogue with Co-founder & Creative Director
Antti Hinkula

"One critical part of our job was to craft a journey for the customers which would better respond to present and future requirements about good coffee shop experience."

Established in 1891, Fazer Café is considered to be one of Helsinki's finest and most longstanding cafés. *page 038*

Kokoro Moi strove to encapsulate the strong and timeless essence of this local gem by striking a balance between sophistication and comfort.

Two rigid and authoritative fonts are utilised in everything from the logo, menu boards, packaging, to clothing, to wall decor.

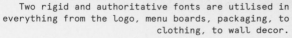

With equal emphasis on both form and function, Melbourne-based interior design studio We Are Huntly prides themselves on their craftsmanship. The team's keen eye for detail communicates a tactfulness that has brought their studio to the forefront of design. They have worked on a diverse range of projects across retail, hospitality, commercial and residential spaces. With every project they apply their name to, We Are Huntly strives to construct a unique space that will both surprise and inspire.

EXPERT TALK ON
INTERIOR BRANDING

We Are Huntly

Dialogue with Co-founders
Kylie Dorotic & Alicia McKimm

What makes a welcoming and interesting café and what makes a boring one?

A welcoming café is defined by a space that people like to sit and spend time in. A space that is considered, inspiring and warm. A boring café is one that lacks atmosphere.

How would a well-executed interior enhance one's coffee experience, especially in Melbourne?

A good coffee experience is as much about a barista who remembers your coffee order and an enjoyable environment to wait in as it is about the coffee. With coffee ingrained in their local culture, Melbournians enjoy a non-fussy environment and generally look for something relaxed and casual, inviting and familiar for social catch-up and as an escape. Through the use of materials, layout, lighting and overall tone, a well-executed interior establishes the café to be warm and approachable, encouraging the patron to stay longer.

What are the points of note when you design the interior of a café?

The key elements to consider are function, layout, number of seats, a good understanding of the kitchen requirements and food offered. Form follows function. Therefore, once the above are established we look to design a warm space that responds to the brand and client's brief. In a city dotted with quality cafés and coffee shops like Melbourne, the interior design of the café has to be memorable enough to give people a reason to travel and experience the space.

What comes to your immediate attention when you were briefed about The Penny Drop project?

It is critical to consider all aspects, from each design element's impact on the user experience to the overall ambience of the space. Spatial planning, the selection of materials, appropriate height and proportion, form and scale, lighting and furniture selection all combined to make for a good interior at The Penny Drop.

How do The Penny Drop's interior design respond to its locale, clientele and food?

Our aim for The Penny Drop was to create a memorable and approachable place on Box Hill. The interior design was a direct response to the concept of 'penny dropping' from the pockets of the Australian Tax Office located above. This is manifested through form, Art Deco references and warm textured surfaces. The curved form of the bar and seating layout that surrounds it echo the 'ripple effect', the same effect the owners hoped The Penny Drop would have on Box Hill and its residents. The design approach was also driven by function. A transitional space was created through zoning and spatial planning. We offer flexibility by a combination of seating zones that cater for individuals as well as larger groups. The coffee counter at the entrance captures the morning and lunchtime takeaway rush, whereas the central dining zone forms a more intimate space to dine. The low seating to the perimeter of the store activates the shop front and provides a place for the individual, while a communal table is set up for groups and overspill.

How did you and Pop & Pac craft an interior and graphic identity that successfully complement each other?

The design process between Pop & Pac and We Are Huntly was seamless. One influenced the other and continued to flow in that direction. From the very beginning we both had a similar response to the "Penny Drop" concept, tapping into an Art Deco reference and working together to establish a colour palette that was suited to both the graphics and interior.

"A good coffee experience is as much about a barista who remembers your coffee order and an enjoyable environment to wait in as it is the coffee."

THE DAY'S DEALS

THE PENNY HAS DROPPED

LIQUID ASSETS FROM THE BAR
PRETTY PENNY BERRY MOJITO

The Penny Drop is an all-day eatery located East of Melbourne's central business district. *page 172*

The seating layout echoes the 'ripple effect' that the café wishes to have on its locale and residents of Box Hill.

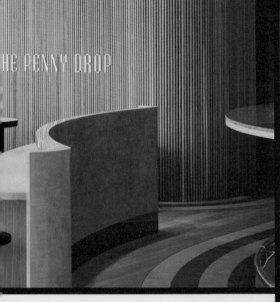

A circular theme is embodied throughout the space.

Branding of the café-restaurant plays with the concept of 'penny dropping' from the pockets of the new Australian Tax Office above it.

Spherical lighting fixtures, round mirrors and a large curved bar all come together as a direct response to the idea of 'penny dropping'.

What makes a good café interior?

From its materials applied to its signage system and the atmosphere, every element should add up to the true story about the owners and their products. A good café interior should also provide plenty of space for deep breathing and is easy to understand, with furniture that meets ergonomic standards.

What are the points of note when it comes to designing a café's interior these days? What do your clients look for in your design?

Our clients generally know about our style and like our work before they come to us. For us it is important to create narrative designs. We would also add touches of humor into our solutions.

The Blue Cup is already famous when they asked for a brand overhaul. What do you want to achieve in this project?

First of all, I want to say that the client has given us 100% of trust when they assign us to do the job. This was the main source of inspiration - the absence of restrictions. The key idea in the initial concept for The Blue Cup was to build an environment upon the image of an elk drawn from our lighting collection. Our client and their customers readily accepted the idea, but it took us two more months to rethink and complete the concept. After the café reopened, some of their customers said they had a hard time forgetting the forest heroes after their visits.

Do you often collaborate with artists on your projects?

The Blue Cup was the second time I proposed to work with an artist. Right now almost all my new projects feature artist collaborations.

What was it like to co-create Café L'étage with LoftBuro?

I have known Oleg Volosovskiy, the director and chief architect of Loftburo studio for more than nine years when we teamed up for the job. We are very good friends, so it was very easy to work together. Everyone was in a right place because we know exactly the kind of skills each other possesses. On this project we had gathered a team of six, including two lead designers, three draftsman and one architect.

There are a lot of mix and match throughout the place. What do you want to convey with these elements?

More than often we source and acquire furniture pieces around the world and combine the collection with local production. Café l'Etage is an exemplar of this approach. The concept of l'Etage's interior underlines the French cuisine they offer and hence, the wall of animal heads crafted out of papier mâché. Since the restaurant has a reasonably priced menu and design that caters for a wide range of guests, we also act in one accord in our approach. By melding incompatible materials, such as marble and a chandelier made from newspaper, we resembled the kind of charm unique to the typical French restaurants.

———

Kleydesign

———

Dialogue with Co-founder Yova Yager

Kleydesign is far from your regular design studio. With projects full of humour and self-irony, they have featured in competitions, exhibitions and lectures, shot videos and featured in design magazines—and that's just the crust of it. In recent years, the studio has focused its activities on interior design for restaurants, bars and cafés. With a passion for experimenting with materials, they apply this fervently within interior spaces, decoration, product design and art installations. Founded by Yova Yoger and Ira Miller in Ukraine in 2008, this multi-talented duo has always stayed true to their motto: "We don't apply for genius, just create the mood."

At Café L'étage, overhanging light bulbs of different sizes tastefully highlight the interior, boosting visual interest and enhancing the café's dynamism. *page 236*

At The Blue Cup, Kleydesign and Nastya Ptichek together brought to life a herd of the country's endangered species across the coffee shop's walls. *page 232*

Vibrant colours and lighting fixtures brighten up the basement café.

"Every element should add up to the true story about the owners and their products. A good café interior should also provide plenty of space for deep breathing and is easy to understand, with furniture that meets ergonomic standards."

The wooden ceiling, tiles and textured wall add visual interest to a room with a limited view.

Biography

485 Design

485 Design is an award-winning agency with a team of passionate designers and creative thinkers that love to push boundaries. They see design not as an appendage of business but an integrated, strategic, and vital component to drive brand value and propel businesses to be more relevant.

6B

6B is a design studio based in Osaka, Japan. They work on all things creative such as advertisements, promotional videos, website design, spacial design and graphic design.

A Friend of Mine

A Friend of Mine, run by Suzy Tuxen, is a holistic design practice based in Melbourne. They work across a mix of industry sectors and design disciplines, adapting creative thinking to varied budgets. They develop brand identities, signage, responsive websites and everything in between.

ACRE

Co-founded in 2011 by TY Zheng and Jason Song, ACRE is a multidisciplinary design house focusing on branding, experience, space and product design. Their methodology melds chaotic exploration and scientific refinement. Every idea proposed passes through their own internal process of cognitive sense and functional aesthetics creating brands that possess cut-through, consistency and consumer recall.

Aerogram Studio

Aerogram Studio is the international design partnership of Tess Golden and Vera Henco, who met while studying design in New York in 2009. While they don't share a studio space, they do share a love of good design, a belief that two heads are better than one, and an obsession with Japanese ramen. Tess is based in Ann Arbor, Michigan, and Vera is based in Düsseldorf, Germany.

Backbone Branding

Backbone is an independent branding studio and creative business partner for clients who is ready for extraordinary solutions. To deliver such solutions they dig deep into a brand's essence and values, clearly understand them, and then inject them into the design. This is the surest way to move beyond design for design's sake and give consumers a brand that is both undeniably relevant and incredibly engaging. The thrill of working with clients to try and tackle increasingly challenging branding problems that then lead to successful businesses is what gets them up in the morning.

Baranova, Asya

Asya Baranova is an architect based in Saint Petersburg, Russia. She graduated with a degree in Architecture from Saint Petersburg State University of Architecture and Civil Engineering in 2013. She worked in architectural studio Form Bureau in Moscow and also co-founded independent publishing house print-o-holic in 2011.

Besze, Judit

Judit Besze is a Budapest-based freelance graphic designer who studied graphic design in an autodidactic way. Her work is her passion. She loves that she can work with people from all around the world and lucky enough to have worked on really different projects in which each of them is a new challenge. Her favourite field is food packaging design. Beyond that she always loves to work on café, bakery and restaurant branding.

Bond Creative Agency

Bond helps new businesses and brands get started. They refresh and revolutionise existing ones for growth. Their services include identity, digital, retail and spatial, as well as packaging and product design. Bond brings together talent from different fields to create cross-disciplinary solutions for brands. Their working model is agile and designer-driven. They have studios in Helsinki, Abu Dhabi and London.

Character San Francisco

Character is a San Francisco-based branding and design agency with a passion for launching, rejuvenating and propelling brands. Their goal is to create lasting and meaningful relationships between their clients' brand and their audience through smart thinking and thoughtful design. They aim to do this by crafting stories that touch people on a personal level, sparking a change in their everyday behavior.

COMMUNE

COMMUNE is a creative team based in Sapporo, Japan specialising in graphic design. Motivated by the will to make things better, COMMUNE works to encourage people and the society for a change. At times, their creations take people by surprise, awakening their emotions, or even moving them to tears.

Content Design Lab

Content Design Lab is a multidisciplinary design and communication agency based in Paris and Bordeaux. Their approach is that of an passionate, open-minded and curious artist/craftsman who considers each new project without preconceived ideas or processes. They build teams of designers, photographers, web developers, motion-designers, typographers, interior designers and much more to craft together contemporary design and communication solutions for people, brands and corporations.

Deux et Quatre

Deux et Quatre is a graphic design studio based in Quebec. Founded in 2013, the team specialises in creating innovative brands and helping clients push their brands forwards with simple but effective communication tools.

filthymedia

Established in 2004 by Joe Pilbeam and Steve Gotts, filthy is a boutique design agency based in Brighton. The studio focus is brand identity, graphic design and art direction for digital, print and website design. Through close collaboration with clients they build long-lasting relationships, creating consistent visual language that enables them to truly connect with their audience. With a passion for design and acute attention to detail from concept to delivery, filthy believes you can have it all.

Firebelly Design

Firebelly works to inspire conscious thought and action through design. They've pioneered an ethic that values honesty, empathy and Good Design for Good Reason™ since 1999. Their clients include public and private sector companies, well-established organisations and ambitious start-ups, each benefits from their proven expertise in conceptualising and delivering beautiful, effective design.

Giraudi Group

Giraudi is based in Monaco and is made up of various companies in meat import/export, restaurant and lifestyle sectors. Today, Giraudi owns six restaurants in the Principality of Monaco and as many abroad. Their philosophy is to create and develop innovative concepts and products.

Infinito Consultores

To create unique and relevant concepts, Infinito combines the clarity of rigorous thoughts with the courage of bold ideas. They are passionate about design and branding, and enjoy helping their clients create and build brands that are relevant and loved. Started in 2005, Infinito is now formed by over thirty talented professionals that work daily towards the objective to become the best brand and strategic design consultancy in Peru.

INNARCH

INNARCH is an architectural and design firm based in Pristina. Founded by Visar Geci and Gezim Kastrati, the team consists of Amir Azemi, Arben Islami, Fjollë Godanca and Taulanta Mjeku. INNARCH's architectural approach is headed towards transformation of utopian ideas into form and function, which is realised over a wide range building types from cultural, residential to commercial.

Kit and Ace

Kit and Ace has built a brand around making meaningful relationships and championing local collaboration, and nowhere is this philosophy more apparent than the branded coffee shop Sorry Coffee Co. Designed to fuel creativity, Sorry was constructed as a space for people to collaborate and ideate, with local artists invited to design signature cups every quarter. As an extension of Kit and Ace, Sorry encapsulates all that the company holds dear — it is irreverent, fiercely focused on quality and proudly Canadian.

Kleydesign

Kleydesign is co-founded in 2008 by Ukrainian designers Yova Yager and Ira Miller. They create space, decoration, product design and art installations. Their favorite is to design and produce product design for the interiors, and to experiment with the quality and the properties of different materials. They don't apply for genius, just create the mood. Humour and self-irony are the main components of their projects.

Kokoro & Moi

Kokoro & Moi is a full-service creative agency transforming brands with bold ideas and progressive concepts. They are always asking questions, challenging norms and piecing together new worlds to solve tasks in unique ways. They create authentic and innovative strategies, craft imaginative solutions and make an impact in the required media — from print and digital to products and environments.

Korolos

Korolos Ibrahim is a Sydney-based freelance designer specialising in strategic branding, creative direction and graphic design. He believes that creatives have the tendency to see or envision beyond what the average eye can see. Their visual but analytical mind aspires to pertain all elements and principles of design. What makes each one of them different is the implementation of strategy and design in today's marketplace.

Lu, Jiani

Jiani Lu is a multidisciplinary graphic designer and photographer born in China. She grew up in Berlin and now lives and works out of Toronto, Canada, where she received her Bachelors in Design at York University/Sheridan College. Her work takes on a simplistic, minimalistic and understated tone that transfers across print design, branding and package design.

Manual

Manual is a design and branding studio based in San Francisco. They help clients express themselves and their products through iconic brand identities and beautiful experiences. Their work strives to clarify purpose, build meaning, and stirs up curiosity and emotion. Manual is founded by in 2009 by Tom Crabtree, who began his career in London working for leading design studios with clients in art, architecture, fashion, and music. He relocated to San Francisco to join Apple's design team, working on packaging design and art direction before starting Manual.

Mimosa Architekti

Mimosa Architekti designs houses outside of banality. They dream them up and think them out, down to the last detail. They are well aware of the responsibility for their common environment, clients' expectations and sources invested in the construction and do not feel sorry about efforts exerted to verify their ideas.

Mind Design

Mind Design is an independent graphic design studio based in East London. The studio was established in 1999 by RCA graduate Holger Jacobs and specialises in the development of visual identities which includes print, web, packaging, signage and interior graphics. Their approach combines hands-on craftsmanship, conceptual thinking and most importantly, intuition. Visual ideas are often developed on the basis of research into production processes or the use of unusual materials.

moodley brand identity

Established in 1999, moodley brand identity is an owner-led, award-winning strategic design agency with offices in Vienna, Graz and Shanghai. They believe their key contribution is to analyse complex requirements and develop simple, smart solutions with emotional appeal — whether corporate or startups, product launch or brand positioning.

Oddds

Oddds was established in 2013 by Reinold Lim from Penang and Sarah Tan from Singapore. Their beliefs revolve around the notion of The New Anthropology, and their work significantly reflects on behaviours and futurism. Oddds' main focuses are in branding, art direction and design.

Onasup & Anzi

Onasup & Anzi are graphic designers based in Seoul and met in university. They seldom collaborate together and OKTOKKI The Café is the best of their several joint projects.

page 164-165

Ong, Elita

Elita Ong has a Masters in Architecture from National University of Singapore and a Diploma in Interior Architecture and Design. She kicked off her career in the architecture firm K2LD and went on to start her own interior design practice that specialises in F&B and hotel spaces. She now resides and leads the interior arm of Foreign Policy Design Group.

page 228-231

OOZN

OOZN is a Singapore-based design studio specialising in architecture, interiors, landscape and masterplanning. Founded in 2013 by Rafal Kapusta and Stephanie Gunawan, OOZN believes in simple hardworking solutions that enhance existing assets whilst ensuring that their work brings a sense of joy and excitement to any situation.

page 252-255

Orka Collective

Orka Collective was founded in 2010 as a project of two independent graphic designers, Ksenia Stavrova from Saint Petersburg and Anton Abo from Kiev. Orka means energy in Icelandic and also sounds like the name of Orca the whale, which they love. They do graphic and editorial design, branding and visual identity, working with clients from different parts of the world.

page 198-203

Petr Kudláek / Lilkudley

Petr Kudláek a.k.a. Lilkudley is a freelance graphic designer, art director and Bull Terrier lover based in Prague, Czech Republic. He loves to work on print and digital projects for small and established clients. He likes to be under control in the full creative process from custom illustrations, logotypes, typography to the layout and animation concept of responsive website.

page 138-139

Phaedrus Studio

Phaedrus is a boutique design studio working across disciplines to design and create objects, spaces, and architecture. Through playful exploration and guided collaboration, they strive to reveal unexpected solutions that could not have been imagined. The studio is founded by David Grant-Rubash, who has built a reputation for his purposeful and playful designs over a wide range of projects from furniture, installations, residential to mixed-use office towers.

page 192-195

Pokorsky, Nikolay

Pokorsky was born in Saint Petersburg in 1990. He graduated from the Faculty of Architecture at Saint Petersburg State University of Architecture and Civil Engineering in 2013 and now works independently on architectural and interior design projects.

page 198-203

Pop & Pac

Pop & Pac is a graphic design studio based in Melbourne. Bespoke, modern, timeless, clever and unique are words that in part, form their design ethos. They don't only seek to create design but consider all their creative executions to be holistically experiential, they connect brand to architecture, web to printed collateral and all of this connects to their clients' stories.

page 064-067, 172-183

Post Projects

Post Projects is a branding and design agency working for small, medium and large organisations across a diverse range of platforms and disciplines.

page 092-093, 208-211

Re-public

Re-public is a graphic design agency specialising in visual identity and communication design. Their work gives new life to brands, and help people communicate effectively. They offer creative services, concepts and strategies across all media and communication channels, putting as much value on selecting the right typeface and paper quality, as they do on implementing new digital media as a natural part of the solution.

page 084-087

Rice Creative

Rice Creative is a branding and creative agency set up in Ho Chi Minh City, Vietnam in 2011 by Joshua Breidenbach and Chi-An De Leo. Out of huge global branding and advertising agencies respectively, the duo sought a smaller, more personal environment to offer world-class creative solutions with emphasis on well-informed concept to a new set of clients. The agency has also engaged with like-minded start-up companies including Marou Faiseurs de Chocolat, to give them voice and visual identity.

page 160-163

Robot 3 Design

Robot 3 Design is founded in 2011 by Fei Pan, who graduated from the Academy of Arts & Design in Tsinghua University.

page 248-251

Schemata Architects

Jo Nagasaka established Schemata Architects right after graduating from Tokyo University of the Arts in 1998. He established the shared creative office "HAPPA" in 2007. Currently he has an office in Aoyama, Tokyo. Jo has extensive experience in a wide range of expertise from furniture to architecture. His design approach is always based on 1:1 scale, regardless of what size he deals with. He works extensively in Japan and around the world, while expanding his design activity in various fields.

page 220-223

Shore

Shore is a full-service design studio in Seattle. Their goal is to express the unique personality of their clients through exceptional design and web experiences. They focus on building brands from the ground up, and taking established brands to new territories. They believe open dialogue and collaboration with their clients is the key to lasting and gratifying assignments. They are an intentionally small studio — each partner is an active practitioner and crafts the work they do.

page 098-099

Studio Esteta

Founded in 2015, Studio Esteta works across a diverse range of architecture and interior projects, specialising in residential, hospitality and retail design under the guidance of Directors Felicity Slattery and Sarah Cosentino. Studio Esteta is dedicated to unique, responsive and inspiring design solutions, with projects focusing on the experiential quality of architecture and space, and how people interact with and experience them.

page 052-055

Studio Juju

Studio Juju is led by Timo Wong and Priscilla Lui to practice design across disciplines of furniture, product and space. The studio's approach is fresh and optimistic, with each project a union of simplicity and warmth, functionalism and whimsy, refinement and relevance. Timo and Priscilla consider their design practice as a medium for collaboration that encourage freedom in exploration.

page 224-227

Studio Mast

Studio Mast is an identity-focused design studio based in Denver, Colorado. They love to tell unique stories by pairing beautiful images with relevant messages.

page 106-107

studioVASE

StudioVASE considers light as the frame of a space, first and foremost. They believe it is essential for a pleasant user experience and good packaging design to complement the values inherent to the brand. They create a new sense of balance on experiencing a physical space through the integration of a variety of fields including integrated branding and art.

page 240-243

Techn Architecture + Interior Design

Techn Architecture + Interior Design is a dynamic and experienced commercial practice led by Directors Nicholas Travers and Justin Northrop, who are passionate about architecture. Founded in 2002, Techn has quickly built an impressive portfolio across a broad section of project types including hospitality, single and multi-residential, commercial, automotive and retail.

page 204-207

The brandbean

The brandbean is an integrated agency with expertise in growing brands in Latin America and around the world. They are a boutique consultancy, with the three partners work personally on every project from concept to delivery. Hilary and Santiago run a unique team combining their strategic experience in the UK with the creative talent of Buenos Aires. They explore, they innovate, they plan, they design, they grow brands. www.thebrandbean.com

The Lab Saigon

A design consultancy and studio in Saigon, Vietnam. The Lab Saigon provides graphic design, interior design, product design, advertising services, and more. They also own a co-working space, three cafés, and a breakfast bar.

The Studio

The Studio combines marketing and design to help brands define their positions, creating a unique voice and building sustainable value. They specialise in brand strategy, identity, packaging, digital design and retail environments. With their founders coming from the two seemingly contradictory backgrounds, every project The Studio undertakes put equal emphasis in artistic values, which make the design unique and memorable, and marketing dimension, which makes their work relevant and commercially viable.

Way of Difference Ltd.

WOD is an up-and-coming design agency in Hong Kong. Their creative and experienced team is devoted to provide a holistic solution to marketing, branding, exhibition and promotion demands with their expertise in design, art direction, exhibition and media strategies. They bring inspiration to clients, and awareness to the public.

We Are Huntly

We Are Huntly is dedicated to bringing something exclusive to each project, be it a custom print, a tailored tabletop, or the fixtures they choose for a bathroom sink. They focus on the details. After all, that's what makes up the bigger picture. Their emphasis on craftsmanship means they select everything not only on form, but also on function. Working across retail, hospitality, commercial, residential and multi-residential, they are not going to design something they wouldn't live in, work in, shop or eat in.

Werklig

Werklig is an independent brand design agency founded in 2008. Their office is located in Helsinki, but they serve more than 50 clients in Finland and around the world. They are designers, creatives and consultants — but most of all, they are problem solvers. They help their clients to turn ideas, products, and services into brands that stand out. They make cost efficient solutions that increase sales, increase brand value and build sustainable customer loyalty.

ZEALPLUS

Founded in 2005, ZEALPLUS is a design studio based in Osaka, Japan. The studio's work is based on a communication design approach that focuses on both graphic and web design.

Acknowledgements

We would like to thank all the designers and companies who have involved in the production of this book. This project would not have been accomplished without their significant contribution to the compilation of this book. We would also like to express our gratitude to all the producers for their invaluable opinions and assistance throughout this entire project. The successful completion also owes a great deal to many professionals in the creative industry who have given us precious insights and comments. And to the many others whose names are not credited but have made specific input in this book, we thank you for your continuous support the whole time.

Future Editions

If you wish to participate in viction:ary's future projects and publications, please send your website or portfolio to submit@victionary.com